100 ways to hear
Good
News

Words of Jesus to encourage and inspire

GERALD O'MAHONY

First published in 2000 by
KEVIN MAYHEW LTD
Buxhall, Stowmarket
Suffolk IP14 3BW

0 1 2 3 4 5 6 7 8 9

ISBN 1 84003 656 7
Catalogue No 1500395

Cover design by Jonathan Stroulger
Edited by Katherine Laidler
Typesetting by Louise Selfe
Printed and bound in Great Britain

Contents

Introduction   7

1   The Good News (I)   11
2   The Good News (II)   12
3   'Well pleased'   13
4   'My Father!'   14
5   If they all sailed away . . .   15
6   Ambassadors   16
7   Reach for the sky   17
8   Turn round where you are   18
9   'Your sins are forgiven'   19
10 The old monk   20
11 Follow conscience   21
12 Heaven my inheritance   22
13 Good parenting   23
14 God is always patient and kind   24
15 God does not boast, God is not arrogant   25
16 God is never envious   26
17 God does not insist on his own way   27
18 God is not irritable or resentful   28
19 God does not rejoice in wrongdoing
       but rejoices in the truth   29
20 God is always ready to excuse   30
21 God who is love never ceases to be love   31
22 No strings   32
23 Symphony in four movements   33
24 Hosepipe   34
25 True direction   35
26 Zacchaeus   36

27	The passwords	37
28	Unbreakable	38
29	Unshakeable	39
30	The Stronger One	40
31	Divine Jesus	41
32	No competition	42
33	The naughty child	43
34	Seek, and you will find	44
35	The character of baptism	45
36	'All sins are forgiven'	46
37	Reconciliation	47
38	Before and after time	48
39	Reality is friendly	49
40	We recognise truth	50
41	The love I mean	51
42	'My favour rests on you'	52
43	With God, no might-have-beens	53
44	Our God, a Trinity of love	54
45	Grace comes *gratis*	55
46	Jesus the Good Samaritan	56
47	Even the unforgivable	57
48	Mark: healing comes first	58
49	Mark: feeding comes next	59
50	Mark: then comes recognition	60
51	Mark: way of the cross	61
52	Mark: the chalice	62
53	Manifesto (Martin Luther)	63
54	'We are merely servants'	64
55	Good News in Paul (I)	65
56	Good News in Paul (II)	66
57	One great commandment	67
58	'My burden is light'	68

59	Forgiving is a joy	69
60	Forgive yourself	70
61	The two sides of the gospel	71
62	We still need to ask for forgiveness	72
63	After Bishop Berkeley	73
64	Why is mine a plank?	74
65	God is simple	75
66	The veil torn, seven freedoms	76
67	Friends do not cause needless pain on purpose	77
68	No taxes for the children	78
69	Not Hagar's children	79
70	The woman at the well	80
71	The Resurrection convergence	81
72	More about the Resurrection	82
73	Even those who think themselves unforgivable	83
74	The beloved disciple	84
75	'All my love, Mum'	85
76	Good News for saints?	86
77	Virtues and vices	87
78	God loves us one at a time	88
79	'This is the word of the Lord about ....' (I)	89
80	'This is the word of the Lord about ....' (II)	90
81	'This is the word of the Lord about ....' (III)	91
82	The jigsaw puzzle	92
83	Treasure in the field	93
84	Pearl of great price	94
85	'Do not be afraid'	95
86	'Ah, but what about . . . ?'	96
87	Field with corn and weeds	97
88	The third man	98
89	The kingdom of forgiveness	99
90	A hundredfold	100

91	The narrow gate	101
92	Dictators and despots	102
93	Why then be good?	103
94	'Didn't God create the devil?'	104
95	Judas	105
96	The sheep and the goats	106
97	Chorazin, Bethsaida and Capernaum	107
98	Ten bridesmaids	108
99	The wedding garment	109
100	Better believe it	110

Introduction

All my life I have noticed that Christians tend to play down the Good News from God which Jesus of Nazareth brought us. Many indeed have tried to turn it into bad news for me; others have allowed it to be 'fairly good news', or 'news that is sometimes good', or 'good news on the way, coming soon', or 'news that is good so long as you are behaving yourself'. I, for one, cannot guarantee good behaviour, so that kind of news would not be good enough for the likes of me.

When news comes from afar, one obvious feature of it is that I cannot change it by my behaviour, good or bad. If the news is good, then the news is good, even if I, at this end of things, am less than good. It is not in my power to turn the Good News into something less than good, or something other than new. It lies out of my reach. When Sir Edmund Hillary and Tenzing Norgay were the first to climb Mount Everest and come back safely, that was quite simply the news, even if I personally never even got out of bed that day.

For the past forty years I have been trying to state the Good News clearly and simply, in ways that nobody can miss. Not everybody welcomes it even then: after all, Jesus was killed for announcing it in the first place. But even people of good will do seem to slide back from it, not daring to speak the whole truth plainly enough.

Besides the Good News being good, it has to be new. The New Testament story must mean that Jesus brought something startlingly new. So often I have heard sayings and teachings dating from before Jesus Christ being labelled as good news, without it being made clear who it was turned it into something good and something new, and how he did so. Just because God blessed the citadel of Zion three thousand years ago, it by no means follows that God meant those same blessings for me in Britain in the twenty-first century after Christ . . . unless we understand reality the way Jesus taught us to.

There is another meaning of 'new' in the Good News, namely that here is a truth not just new in its time but new today, and new for ever. It comes to us as the cure and antidote of our fallen nature, so there is usually a passage of time in the case of even the best of human beings before the Good News is really heard and hits home. We do not start out on our lives aware of our need of relief: I myself was 24 years old and already a student for the priesthood before I knew what the News really was. I learnt it just in time.

Human nature is slow to understand God's goodness, and that is really my reason for trying to express the news from God in a hundred different ways. If I had the time and skill I would express it in a thousand and one different ways, in the hope that at least one of the ways would come home to the heart of a reader, and lead him or her to see the force of the other thousand. We usually recognise the wonderful truth first of all in one particular area of our lives. From then on, nothing in our lives is ever quite the same again; but still the truth, like yeast in the dough, takes time to enter every other corner of our lives and transform the whole person.

For it is the News that transforms. I am sometimes criticised for going on about a message, as if I should really be going on about behaviour. Only when the human race opens its ears and eyes and hands to the message from outside will our behaviour change, for better and for good.

I know there will be a reaction against the title of this little book. Many will say the notion of Good News has been done to death; everything was 'Good News' for years after the Second Vatican Council, and now the general public needs a rest from it. Unfortunately the general public, by and large, still does not know what the real Good News is. Only today, as I write this, someone who has been for the past thirty years a most generous Religious care-worker told me she was delighted to hear for the first time, when I said it, that heaven is a gift and not something that has to be earned. If this can happen in the green wood, surely the dry wood also needs telling?

St Paul urges Timothy to proclaim the message in season and out of season, whether the time is favourable or unfavourable (see 2 Timothy 4:2).

Anyone who has heard me preach or teach, or who has read books or articles I have written in the past, will recognise here the same beautiful themes – beautiful with a beauty coming not from me, needless to say – sometimes told in the ways I have told them before, and sometimes, I hope, in new ways.

And one word of warning: this is a book for sinners. The virtuous may not like it.

About the author

Gerald O'Mahony is a Jesuit priest, who has worked as a teacher and an adviser to teachers of religion, and who for the past sixteen years has been a retreat director and writer at Loyola Hall Spirituality Centre, Rainhill, near Liverpool. He says of himself that he was 24 years old – after twelve years of Catholic schooling and five years as a student for the priesthood – before he heard the Good News clearly for the first time. He has never looked back.

Acknowledgements

I am always grateful to my family for the unconditional love which they have given me. Among my teachers of religion when I was young I would especially like to remember here Joan Higham in my primary school who taught me to pray at all times, George Walkerley SJ my novice master, and Tom Gornall SJ who taught me about natural theology.

Pages 89-91 are straight quotations from three pages devised by Brian Grogan SJ, which he has kindly and generously allowed me to use in any way I wished.

The quotation on page 63 is from Luther's *Primary Works*, edited by Henry Wace and Carl A. Buchheim (Murray, 1883).

The quotations on page 69 are from *Seventy times Seven* by Gerald O'Mahony SJ (Mayhew McCrimmon, 1977, pages 13 and 19).

The quotation on page 99 is from the same book, page 10.

The reference on page 104 is to *Concise Theological Dictionary*, Karl Rahner and Herbert Vorgrimler (Herder/Burns and Oates, 1965).

1

The Good News (I)

The first public act of Jesus was to go and be baptised by John the Baptist. Then, so the gospels tell us, he went into Galilee, proclaiming the Good News from God. 'The time has come,' he said. 'The kingdom of God is near. Repent and believe the Good News!' What was the Good News? Not simply the fact that the kingdom of God was near: John had already preached that message, and he was not the bringer of the Good News.

The only news from God that the gospels have given us at this stage of the story is the news that Jesus is the beloved Son of God and that God is well pleased with him. That word, and the Spirit appearing like a dove, came from heaven, and both the word and the dove are Good News.

To begin with, the news seems to be chiefly good for Jesus; but after his struggle with temptation he is beginning to invite his hearers to see themselves as his younger brothers and sisters, so that his baptism becomes ours as well if we want it. The heavens are split open above us, and the dove comes down on us, to say that the flood of God's anger is all over, an olive branch is held out to us, and life will begin afresh. Above all, God is saying to each human being who can hear it, 'You are my beloved son . . .', or 'You are my beloved daughter: with you I am well pleased.'

To repent as Jesus asks is simply to open our ears to the invitation he extends. John's baptism was a necessary prelude to hearing Jesus, because those who went to be baptised by John were admitting they were sinners and in need of help. The help Jesus offers is way beyond anything anyone had dared to hope for.

2
The Good News (II)

As a result of the Good News I may at any time say to God, 'I am your beloved son; with me you are well pleased.' Any girl or woman may say to God, 'I am your beloved daughter; with me you are well pleased.' Other translations of the word from God would describe God as saying, 'My favour rests on you.' In either case, the being 'well pleased' or the 'favour' do not go away; they are permanent. Like the rainbow telling Noah that now the dove of peace has come there will be no more anger from God, so the baptism of Jesus is a sign of permanent acceptance of each human being as a first-generation child.

Noah's dove was a promise; Jesus' dove is the fulfilment.

Why turn the gospel phrases round? Why do I not simply imagine God saying to me, 'You are my beloved son . . . '? Now this may be a personal view, but to hear God saying, 'Gerald, you are my beloved son' takes imagination. I am imagining something true, but I am imagining. Whereas if I say, 'I am Gerald your beloved son . . .', then I can hear my own voice; I am not imagining anything. I am making a response in faith to what God is all the time saying to me.

For me the enormous blessing of being able to make such an assertion is that I can counteract anything that goes wrong in my life. If I make a fool of myself, I can remind myself that I am still God's beloved, and that is the only thing that really matters. Similarly, if I have done something downright harmful, my God hates what I have done but still loves me. If I do something well, reminding myself that I am God's son reminds me also where the power to do well comes from.

3

'Well pleased'

How could God be well pleased with me, such a sinner, such a failure in so many ways? When I was a little boy in primary school, the teachers assured me that when I was first baptised I had as it were a shiny white baptismal robe, not the visible one my family wrapped me up in, but an invisible one. It was beautiful beyond compare. But alas, every time since then that I did anything naughty, my naughty deed put a stain on the beautiful robe. (They then went on to say, that only 'going to confession' could remove the stain, but that is not the present point and will be dealt with later.)

What the baptismal robe actually stands for is something permanent, which no amount of sinning can destroy or spoil. Beauty is in the eye of the beholder, and God beholds me beautiful. God beholds every daughter or son as beautiful. The best illustration I can think of is there in the great paintings of the return of the prodigal son. Rembrandt has two famous ones. In each of them the returning son is a poor scruffy mess with a disreputable past, but the father is clasping him in his arms with an almost blind love. It is not hard to hear the father saying, 'My beloved, my son, I am well pleased with you; I am glad beyond words that you came back. My favour never left you.'

For this relief of the father is not something new. We gather from Jesus' story how the father was on the lookout every hour of every day for the son coming back. The father's love is not only there at the end of the story; his love is the same throughout: 'Where are you, forgetting that I am here for you?' and 'Such joy that you are back!' That moment of reunion is ours for the asking, every hour of every day.

4

'My Father!'

There are two versions of the Lord's Prayer. The one we usually say each day as Christians comes from Matthew's gospel (6:9-13). The other comes from Luke's gospel (11:1-4). Luke's version is shorter and leaves out three important words or phrases. Luke does not say, 'Thy will be done', nor does he say, 'Deliver us from evil', and above all, he does not say, 'Our'. The prayer begins simply 'Father'.

A rabbi would only give his disciples one prayer model of this kind, not two versions. So which is the one Jesus gave? Was it Matthew's, after which the disciples known to Luke dropped these three important aspects? Unthinkable. So it must have been that Jesus taught the version Luke gives us and the disciples added on the rest, from other sayings and actions of Jesus. For instance, having witnessed Jesus praying in the garden of Gethsemane they would want to include 'Thy will be done'. Having each lived with the privilege of calling God 'Abba! Father!' they would begin to say together, 'Our Father'.

Jesus himself, then, taught them, and taught us, to pray, 'Father!', that is, 'My Father!' even before we learn to say, 'Our Father'. Even if the rest of Christendom, even if the rest of the human race, sail away to heaven and leave me behind as not worth taking, I can still cry to God as *my* Father. I do not have to deserve to be called one of 'us' before God will love me.

Anywhere, any time, no matter how alone and lost I feel at the time, I can, with Jesus' blessing and permission, call on God as my very own Father.

5

If they all sailed away . . .

If the whole wide world of people sailed away into eternal bliss and left me behind, would I be alone? If they all decided I was a failure and there was no room for me in the lifeboat, would they be right? We can feel like that sometimes, when everything in our lives seems to be going wrong.

But in that case Jesus would be with me, rather than with those in the boat. Jesus makes his point of view quite plain: 'As long as you did it to the least of my brothers or sisters, you did it to me.' At such a time of unhappiness I qualify as the least of the brothers, so if they all go away and leave me behind, they all go away and leave Jesus behind . . . with me. The boat will have to come back and fetch us; otherwise they will look silly turning up at the gates of heaven without Jesus their saviour.

Peter the apostle boasted to Jesus on the way to the Garden of Gethsemane that if all the others fell away, he would never do such a thing. Within a few hours he had deserted Jesus in his hour of need. The reality was the other way round: Jesus would never desert Peter.

Our first instinct always is to take sayings like that one of Jesus as being a duty: he said that about 'as long as you do it . . .', so therefore I must treat people more carefully. We forget to apply it first to ourselves as extremely Good News.

For the bottom line is that we can all say, 'Jesus will never desert me.'

6

Ambassadors

St Paul tells the Corinthians that he and his friends come to them as ambassadors. God was in Christ, reconciling the world to himself, not holding the faults of human beings against them. God has entrusted to Paul and the other disciples the news that humanity is reconciled.

As followers of Christ, all Christians are ambassadors, entrusted with that Good News, and the first people they should tell it to are themselves. No use my coming as an ambassador to a foreign land to tell the people the great king has freely forgiven them, and then going in fear of my life myself. This Good News is for the ambassadors first: that is why they are ambassadors, they are so delighted with the news that they cannot keep it to themselves.

Telling the listeners in the strange land to 'be reconciled' is the same as telling them 'to repent'. The reconciliation is there already, as far as the great king is concerned. All the hearers have to do is to listen to the news and believe it, then see what a difference it makes to their lives from then on.

The dove who comes in our baptism is the first ambassador, bringing the olive branch from God. Once the coming of the dove has transformed our lives, we will always want to be offering the dove to others. The wind of the Spirit does not blow on me and then stop: it blows through me to reach others. I become like a flute, which when picked up and played attracts the attention of listeners.

7

Reach for the sky

God is always saying, 'Reach for the sky. I will catch you if you fall.' The Good News does not make a person fearful, it frees the one who listens. Once we know that God will continue to love us no matter how well or badly we perform, then we can begin to follow our hearts, the hearts God gave us in the first place.

I am an absolutely hopeless ice-skater, and the reason must be that I have no great sense of balance; nor do I like falling on hard, wet, surfaces. If ice was as soft as a cushion to fall down on, I imagine I would be able to launch out with the best of them. As a child I turned down the opportunity of flying as a passenger in a rickety-looking monoplane at an air show because I did not fancy what would happen if the engine failed. But what a difference if the safety of the plane could have been guaranteed.

The Good News can turn us into great performers, because the guaranteed love from God acts in the way a safety net does for a trapeze artist. It does not make the true listener want to do nothing; it does not make the true listener want to hurt God. It only brings out the best in a listener.

Who would want to do nothing, when a perfect pair of wings was at their disposal? Who would want to hurt God, if they realised all the world and all the universe was theirs as a gift from God? Who would want to hurt God, if they realised God was the one who makes them permanently lovable?

Once God's sky is the limit, we are free to fly in it.

8

Turn round where you are

This is a piece of advice I found years ago in an extract from one of the early Christian writers. I never noted his name, because I was so thrilled with what he was saying. He said that no matter how far we have run away from God, all we have to do to repent is to turn round where we are. We do not have to retrace our steps back along the weary way we have come, in order to find God's love again. I was astonished to read such a message, since at that time I always presumed I would have to sort myself out before God would look at me again.

But no, said this ancient writer, God is always smiling in our direction, and the reason we keep on running away once we have started running away, is that our back is turned to God's welcoming smile. That smile is like the sunshine, so all I can see is darkness and my own shadow mocking me. But if I turn round and look at God, I see that he has never stopped loving me. The light shines on me, and the shadows disappear.

The longer and further I run away, the more my imagination tells me I will have all that way to climb back to find God again. But no, all I have to do is turn round where I am, and the relationship is healed immediately. Then in all humility I can start trying to retrace my steps to a better way of life.

The attempt to improve is not a condition of God's love; it is a consequence of God's love.

9

'Your sins are forgiven'

When Jesus was accused of forgiving sins, thus taking to himself what only God can do, we need to notice what the words of Jesus actually were. To the paralysed man let down on a stretcher through the roof Jesus said, 'Son, your sins are forgiven.' He did not say, 'Son, I forgive your sins.' 'Your sins are forgiven' means, in the idiom of Jesus' native tongue, 'God has forgiven your sins'. This is a reverent way of speaking of God without mentioning the name of God. Using the same idiom, Jesus said to the sinful woman at the house of Simon, 'Your sins are forgiven.' Then he added, 'Your faith has saved you; go in peace.' To the woman who touched his cloak and was cured, Jesus said, 'Your faith has made you well; go in peace.'

To the woman caught committing adultery and brought before Jesus, he simply says, 'Neither do I condemn you. Go, and do not sin again.' It is the Father of Jesus who has forgiven, and so Jesus does not condemn. That is not what he came for. He came to tell us that God's attitude to us is that of the best of fathers and beyond, who will always love the sinful child even while he detests the sin. The paralysed man evidently believed, once told, that he was a son of God and his sins were therefore already forgiven. He was able to believe it, so he got up from his bed of fear and stepped away home to start serving God again. So too the woman who was healed; she was able to believe she was a daughter of God and therefore in no way unclean.

My sins are forgiven, and your sins are forgiven, if we can only believe it.

Our faith does not create the forgiveness: faith simply has the courage to believe that for a son or a daughter of God the forgiveness is always there.

10

The old monk

From one of the collections of stories from abbeys and monasteries long ago comes the story of an old monk who was dying. He had never been a shining light in the abbey: he was always late for things, always untidy, always a bit slovenly in finishing his tasks. He had been known to disappear into the town now and then over the years, reappearing hours later somewhat the worse for wear.

So when he was dying, the other monks gathered round his bed to pray for him, and when he was in his last hour they sent for the Father Abbot. The Abbot came, and was surprised to see that the old monk had a seraphic smile on his face, obviously not in the least afraid of dying. 'How now, Brother?' said the Abbot. 'How is it that after such a lax life as yours you can be so serene at the thought of meeting your Judge in a very short time?'

The old monk replied, 'Ah, you see, Father Abbot, a couple of days ago the good Lord Jesus appeared to me and said, "Dear Brother, you have broken every rule in the book . . . except one. You chose well. You never broke the rule that says: *Judge not, and you will not be judged.* Your brethren all judged you, but you never judged them in return. Therefore I will welcome you straight into Paradise." So you see, Father Abbot, I have nothing to fear.'

And with that, the old monk died, a smile still on his face.

11

Follow conscience

The standard rule about conscience, for Catholics and for Protestants, is that our personal conscience is one of the ways in which God speaks to us. Jesus did not refer to his own 'conscience' using that word, which had not been coined in his day. Instead he spoke about his Father's will, which he found in his own heart as we find it in ours.

Conscience is not about the past; it is about the immediate future. Conscience is my judgement about the rightness or wrongness of the action immediately in front of me. Therefore no one else knows it except me. My parents, my spouse or partner, my children, friends, relations, my parish priest, my vicar, my bishop, the Pope, the government . . . all these can tell me what *they* think I ought to do in the present circumstances. But it stands to reason that the only person who knows what *I* think I ought to do here and now is me . . . and God.

God, moreover, is my Abba, according to Jesus, and will forgive me if I fail to do what I know I ought to do. For a Christian, conscience is not a millstone laid round my neck by others, but an invitation to do great things for God, who will, as I said a few pages back, catch us if we fall.

12

Heaven my inheritance

We do not have to earn heaven. Heaven is our inheritance, and the main thing about an inheritance is that the inheritor does not have to earn it. It just comes to those who wait. The Letter of Paul to the Ephesians, the First Letter of Peter and the Letter to the Hebrews all speak of heaven as our inheritance. St Paul also tells the Ephesians that they have been saved by grace, not by anything that they themselves have done. We find Paul in the Acts of the Apostles saying the same sort of thing, about the promise of our inheritance.

The same theme has been taken up in recent times by the writers of the Roman Catholic eucharistic prayers. Prayer III says, 'May he [Christ] make us an everlasting gift to you [Father] and enable us to share in the inheritance of your saints.' Prayer IV says, 'Father, in your mercy grant also to us, your children, to enter into our heavenly inheritance. . . .'

The idea that we can earn heaven is very tempting to human minds, but is in fact a heresy as far as Christians are concerned, the heresy of Pelagius. The way I was taught as a child was riddled with Pelagianism, and that heresy is very clinging: it gives people guilt-feelings when they try to break free of it. Either that or it leaves behind a residue of competition and anxiety that 'I may not be doing well enough' compared to everyone else.

When Mary in her *Magnificat* sings of being poor, the poverty is not anything to do with money; it is to do with seeing heaven as her inheritance, though she has done nothing of herself to deserve it, since she has nothing of herself. Everything she has is a gift from God.

13

Good parenting

God loves us, not because we are good children, but because we are God's children. Jesus, as God's final messenger, tells us that the best and truest way to think of God is by way of our own experience of good parents. The covenant made with Moses long before Jesus' time was more like the arrangement between an emperor and a subject race. 'Keep the laws of my empire and I will repay you by keeping you safe and prosperous.' When time and again the people broke God's laws, and yet time and again God renewed the covenant, the prophets began to think the covenant was becoming permanent, but they did not know how to express the new covenant. Jesus gave the clue, which no other before or since would have dared to be the first to give: God is first-generation Father to each human person.

In that context, the story of the prodigal son is the story of God's relationship with each sinful human being. All the father wants is to have his son back safe and sound; the adventures the son went through while running away simply do not matter by comparison. Mothers and fathers fret over their children as long as the children are in any kind of trouble. They do not love the children less on that account: if anything, they love them more. And the saying of Isaiah and the saying of the Psalm – that even if a father or a mother did ever forget their child, God would not forget – this is now applied by Jesus in effect not just to the people as a whole but to each poor lost or wayward human being.

I am loved, not because I am good but because I am God's. There is no way I can ever earn a gift like that. God loves me because God wants to, not for anything I have done in the past or will do in the future.

14

God is always patient and kind

God is love, so St John tells us in his First Letter. And love, so St Paul tells us in his First Letter to the Corinthians, is patient and kind. Also, Paul says, love never ends. Add those together and we can say with confidence that God is always patient and kind.

We know what it is like to be treated with patience and kindness when we are slow at learning something, or when we have let somebody down. The patience and the kindness are like a soothing ointment on our hearts: they give us courage to try again. Even those who have had an unhappy childhood know how much they have longed for their elders to be patient and kind with them. The David Copperfields and the Oliver Twists of this world know what they are looking for when they run away from cruelty.

St Paul tells preachers and teachers of the Good News about God to insist on it always, in season and out of season. When St Mark in his gospel tells us about Jesus going to the fig tree out of season and looking for figs, he is telling us a parable, whatever about the poor fig tree with its beautiful leaves. Jesus went on to visit the temple in Jerusalem the same day, and he found that 'out of season' as well, in spite of its beautiful stones and wealth.

Jesus is bringing instead the trees of life that were foretold, which would be fruitful every month of the year; he brings the tree of life that is fruitful in season and out, and a temple that will never be caught unready.

We will never catch God on a bad day, short of kindness or of patience.

15

God does not boast, God is not arrogant

We know this is true because, as before, we know from John that God is love, and from Paul that love is not boastful or arrogant. Why should this be such Good News for us? Well, most people know from dealing with bureaucracy and high-handed officials what a pain it is to be pushed to one side. Such people can, in extreme cases, hold our life and our death in their hands, and if they are more concerned for themselves than for honesty and truth, woe betide us. But God is not like that, quite the contrary. What a relief!

When we look at the beauty and the wonder of the world, and maybe dream our way round the marvellous holiday places we see on television, we never hear God saying, 'Rather nice, isn't it? I suppose you know who created all this?' If I was responsible for the Grand Canyon and the Pacific islands and the stars and the sunsets and the countless millions of other beauties of the earth and the universe, I would certainly let people know. But not a word from God. The prophets remind us where to look and praise, but God is very quiet.

Similarly, all the inspiration behind every work of art . . . we do not think up such things by ourselves. We could not have a single thought in our heads unless it came to us as a gift. We often act as if all these riches came from ourselves alone . . . yet God never butts in to say, 'Excuse me, you are mistaken.'

In the town of Buxton, not far from where I live, there is an unusual museum called a micrarium. Through microscopes and on screens the visitor can see the tiniest plants and live creatures magnified ninety times. Such little wonders are beneath the notice of most of us, but not beneath God's notice.

16

God is never envious

Envy begrudges other people their good fortune, and would like to take it from them and have it instead of them. Since God is there underpinning every thought, word and deed of ours – good, bad or indifferent – and since God is behind every item of life in the whole universe, God could hardly be envious of humans.

But envy is a spoiler, and from spite will often ruin the joy or pleasure of another person. God, therefore, is not like that. Superstition often leads people to fear that when they are happy God is sure to spoil their joy, to bring them down a peg or two. God, however, is not like that. Every sight I see through my two eyes, God underpins and makes possible, so that only God and I know exactly what it looks like. Likewise only God and I know what it feels like when I meet with disappointment. God feels it with me. Love involves pain and loss as well as final joy, and God shares love with me.

When there was an earthquake in 1999 in Turkey which killed 17,000 people, I heard of an atheist crowing, 'Where is your God now?' Well, God is love, and now and then it pays to reverse that sentence and say, 'Love is God'. When an earthquake devastates a whole area there is no love in the earthquake, sure enough, but there is no malice in the earthquake either. The rocks do what rocks do. But there is plenty of love in the situation. There are more than 17,000 people mourning their loved ones because they love and miss them; there are brave rescue workers with no thought for themselves; there are relief agencies ever ready to step in and cope with the most awful situations; there are officials learning the lessons; there are TV viewers grieving and offering help where they can. God is where love is.

17

God does not insist on his own way

Love has its own fixed destination, which is the fullness of joy; but there are many ways to the destination, and God does not insist on his own way. We have only to look again at the story of the prodigal son. The father of the younger son surely never wanted him to leave home. Like most parents he would be willing to let the son go, for the sake of the son's own growth, but it would break his heart as such partings do break the hearts of mothers and fathers alike. And in this case the father might have been having nightmares of shameful and distressing things happening to the son, only too like what the son really was going through. The father wanted the son to come home, but did not insist on the son doing well and then coming home in style. So, too, God does not insist that the only way back to him is by keeping all the rules and regulations, or even by following our conscience.

The story of the ancestors of Jesus gives a similar picture of God. Time and again they went against the genuine vision of God that their best prophets were giving them, but time and again God gave them another chance. When we look into the family tree of Jesus given by Matthew and by Luke, there is a liberal scattering of villains among them, but God never said, 'Enough of this!' and cut the tree down. Evil can never win against love. Evil is so logical, but love has a logic all its own.

God is not sitting there with a blueprint for each of us, with our own name on it, such that when we go off course he despairs of us. God who is love starts today and moves on from there. Wherever I have got myself to, God is there too, and urges me not to look back but to look forward in love.

18

God is not irritable or resentful

To say 'God is not irritable' is almost the same as saying how patient God is. For me a most striking thing is that God gives me life and breath and goes along with everything that I do. In my case, for 65 years God has given me the supplies for my daily life, and yet has never once complained that I was misusing any of the gifts. Plenty of other people have told me from time to time that I was not behaving in a loving or thoughtful way, or even that I was downright wrong in my actions, but never a word from God the provider.

What a wonderful teacher God is, who never shouts or complains. Teachers who are irritable are sure to make their pupils edgy and insecure, but for this 65-year long lesson God has never been other than calm. Some people complain that God is silent; for myself I would prefer that to a god who lectured me at every turn.

God is not resentful, meaning that God does not store up the wrongs we did, to punish us just when we least expect it. Jesus makes it clear in the gospels that bad things that happen to us are not punishments from God. The blindness of the man born blind was nothing to do with whether he or his parents had sinned. The reason the tower at Siloam fell on eighteen unfortunates was nothing to do with their being sinners or not sinners. Presumably the real reason was that the same tower was badly built or falling to ruin. Most clearly of all, Jesus' own death, condemned to the cross as a criminal when he had done everything right and nothing wrong, shows how good and bad fortune in this life are nothing to do with just deserts. God is not sending us trials, but is really helping us to bear them. God's love was what upheld Jesus in his trials.

19

God does not rejoice in wrongdoing but rejoices in the truth

One of the reasons some people are reluctant to accept the Good News from God is that they think they would thereby make God approve of evil. Yet Jesus makes it quite plain that he does not approve of the sin, even when he tells the sinners that they are forgiven. When Jesus sits and eats with the sinners and the tax collectors, he is not afraid of catching sinfulness off their clothes or off their food, as the Pharisees would seem to have been. He greets them as his brothers and sisters, thus showing them they are precious to God, not rejects. This very knowledge helps them to give up their sinful ways.

When the tax collector Zacchaeus is thrilled at being treated as an equal by Jesus, he makes huge promises of amendment. Jesus does not then say to him, 'Oh, no, Zacchaeus; no need to go over the top!' On the contrary, Jesus is delighted, and exclaims that salvation has come to the house that day. When the woman caught committing adultery is left alone with Jesus because all her accusers have belatedly remembered their own sins, Jesus does not simply say, 'Go home', but, 'Go away, and don't sin any more'. This is not putting conditions on the forgiveness: quite clearly if the mob had brought the same woman back the next week with the same accusation, Jesus would not have condemned her then either; but he would have repeated the appeal, 'Don't sin any more'.

The truth, which both Jesus and God his Father rejoice in, is that love and forgiveness are one in God, such that we can say, 'God is love', but equally, 'God is forgiveness'.

20

God is always ready to excuse

St Paul says that love is always ready to make excuses for the loved one. The Greek word he uses means first of all to seal off, to protect, to make watertight, to fend off, to cover, to shelter. Later on, as a metaphor, it can mean to endure. So we may say that God, being love, acts like a waterproof guard all around us in the wet weather, or else makes us a boat that will not let in the sea. The version given in the Jerusalem Bible is fair, saying that God always makes excuses for us. We are leaky boats, but every time we spring a leak God goes in there and makes excuses for us, patches us up again.

We can see God making excuses in the stories Jesus tells. The younger son who comes home with a sorry tale is not even allowed to make his own excuses: the father takes them for granted. The farmer is all for cutting down the fig tree in the vineyard which has been doing nothing for too long, but the landowner says to manure it and give it another year. The other farmers are all for pulling up the weeds even though that might harm the wheat, but the landowner says to let them both grow to the harvest. Jesus' actions show the same willingness to excuse. Peter and the other close disciples who ran away when Jesus was arrested are all given another chance: Jesus excused them even before they ran away, just as he excused Peter before he betrayed his master.

St Paul goes on to say that love bears all things, hopes all things, endures all things. So does God, since God is love. One of the things we make God bear is our resentment. We blame God for all sorts of things that are not the result of love, which God, therefore, cannot be blamed for. We have an unfair version of what it means to say God is 'all-powerful'.

21

God who is love never ceases to be love

We tend to imagine that God has a breaking point. If we test God enough, something is bound to give and we will find ourselves let down by God. For St Paul, however, love never ends. I remember somewhere in my teacher training days hearing that little children round the age of two often go through a stage of being thoroughly nasty, trying the patience of the parents quite openly and on purpose. They are testing to see if they will get thrown out. 'If I do this, will they throw me out? If I do that, will they throw me out? If I do the worst possible thing I can think of, will they throw me out then?' And if the parents survive the test, then the child usually settles down and becomes a respectable citizen again.

St Peter went through the same process with Jesus. No doubt he did not mean to, but after a lot of boasting about his loyalty he did the very worst evil he could ever have imagined for himself. He who was the great leader in his own eyes betrayed Jesus because he followed Jesus into trouble and then had to wriggle his way out again because he was afraid. According to Luke, Jesus was in the background at the time and saw him do it. Either then or later or both, Jesus gently forgave Peter, and what a change in Peter after that: never again was he weak, because he had done the worst possible thing and it had not changed Jesus' love for him.

What the Good News can do for us is to bring forward that 'never ending' aspect of love to the here and now. I believe and I know that even if I did the very worst possible thing I could think of, God would still be love and would still love me. So therefore I have nothing to fear any more.

22

No strings

There are no strings on God's love for us. God makes no conditions before deciding whether to love us or not: the outcome is certain, and is in our favour. Moreover, God has decided to love me, and to love you, whether or not we conform to the rules of those who live around us.

This wonderful truth comes from the Trinity of God itself. The First Person of the Trinity, whom Jesus taught us to call 'Abba! Father!', is the love that had no beginning and no cause. 'I am who I am,' says God to Moses, a God who has no source, no parents, no limit of place or time. God the First Person is the light that nobody lit. In the language of love, the First Person is the love that is simply there, the love that nobody loved first, the love that does not need to have love shown to it before itself loving another.

The Second Person, on the other hand, whom we know in Jesus, is light from light, the reflection of the light, the one in whom we see the light reflected. Christ is love-in-return-for-love, the source of all praise and thanksgiving and gratitude and security. What we see on the cross, if we have eyes to see, is the perfect reflection of the love of the Father: 'I will love you no matter what you do or try to do to me. I will love you even if you crucify me. You cannot stop me from loving you.' In return for the love shown to him from always by his Father, Jesus shows and reflects that same love on to us.

If God the Father, the First Person, was to love me or anyone else because of our beauty or because of our goodness or because of our obedience, that would mean we were the cause of God's love – but that would be nonsense.

23

Symphony in four movements

Life for a Christian is like a symphony in four movements, which can be played over many times. The first movement says, 'God loves me', with no strings. The Holy Spirit comes down on me as at my baptism and reassures me. I am a child of God and as dear to God as any other child.

The second movement is mine: I say, 'I believe'; I believe that God loves me with no conditions, no 'ifs', no 'buts'. I trust that God really loves me and is pleased with me, even when my actions may be pleasing neither to God nor to myself.

In the strength of that belief I find myself wishing to give God love in return. The third movement says, 'God invites me'. Inevitably once a person really understands that love and forgiveness are always to hand, there is a surge of gratitude. Life from then on becomes no longer a life of slavery and fear, but a desire to show gratitude.

The fourth movement is about my love for God. It says, 'I come, because you called me.' Faith is the beginning, the end is love.

The movements must be played in that order. This is the Way of Jesus, to see things in that order. He is from above; his enemies were from below, trying to make God love them.

24

Hosepipe

I often use a metre or so of hosepipe to illustrate the change Jesus made, from the Old Covenant to his New Covenant. Hold the pipe with the loop at the top (∩) and to get water through the pipe it has to be pumped up; this shows how great effort must be made to climb up towards God *before* God's love comes back to the one who worships. It is like trying to breathe out before ever breathing in. Time and time again the prophets before Jesus show God saying, 'If you keep my rules, I will be your God; but if you fail, I will desert you', or words to that effect. It all depends on human effort.

But Jesus turned the whole idea on its head. The best illustration of Jesus' way would be to turn the hosepipe upside down (∪) with the loop at the bottom. God pours in the love from above, and by the grace of God it flows up again on the other side. This can be shown to work as a model: pour water in at one end and it comes out at the other, all by itself! Such is a life lived always in gratitude for the love of God ever coming down. The power of love-in-return is all God's, not ours.

25

True direction

The Holy Spirit of God flows in a certain direction, from the Father to the Son first, then from the Son back to the Father. God the Son who is 'light from light' receives light and then reflects it back. In our own world of the adopted children of God, the Spirit has to come to us before we can reflect it back to God and before we can imitate it by showing God-like love for our fellow human beings. We have to breathe in the breath of God before we can breathe it out.

I have just illustrated how the movement of love is like a symphony in four movements which have to go in a certain direction. I have also given the image of a length of hosepipe held the wrong way up and the right way up. Jesus himself says to his enemies, 'I am from above; you are from below.'

Jesus was going against the flow of the river, the human river. His preaching was completely different from anything that had ever been preached before in the history of the world. By sharing with us his image of God as 'Abba', he set in motion in our world the counter-movement which comes from the Holy Spirit. The current of the previous countless centuries had been to do with human beings getting the gods to fit in with human wisdom. Even among the chosen people of the Jews, once the prophets began to get genuine insights into God's ways, the direction of the current stayed the same as before: 'Now we have clear laws from God: let us keep them, *and then* God will love us and continue to favour us.'

Jesus' enemies faced him in deadly earnest and wanted to stem the new tide he brought. They killed him: but they could not kill divine love.

26

Zacchaeus

The story of Jesus and Zacchaeus as told by St Luke is a perfect example of the way Jesus works. Zacchaeus is a tax collector, a traitor to the Jewish people, an extortioner, and a cheat. Perhaps he is unhappy with his success and ill-gotten gains, but at all events he wants to see this Jesus everyone is talking about. He climbs a tree to get a good view of Jesus coming by, since he himself is a small man and cannot see properly over the heads of the crowd lining the way.

Jesus sees him up the tree, and stops and calls out, 'Come down, Zacchaeus; I am going to dine at your place today.' No conditions, no 'ifs', no 'buts'. Zacchaeus is astonished and delighted. To think that a famous prophet from God should just invite himself like that to a sinner! Jesus did not say, 'If you promise from now on to keep all the ten commandments and the other rules of Moses, I will come to your place.' That would have been normal. Jesus did not say, 'Zacchaeus, if you give half your money to the poor and if you pay back four-fold to anyone you have cheated, I will come and join you in a meal.' If Jesus had said that, Zacchaeus would have run a mile.

But Jesus made no conditions, and Zacchaeus hurried away to prepare the meal, in the middle of which he made his voluntary speech about giving half his money to the poor and paying back four-fold to those he had wronged. His offer was voluntary, and was given in reply to the love-with-no-strings Jesus had shown him on behalf of his Father in heaven.

1. God loves; 2. Zacchaeus believes; 3. God invites; 4. Zacchaeus, inspired by the Spirit, gives *more not less* generously than the law required.

27

The passwords

Jesus, at the Last Supper, referred to the Holy Spirit as the Advocate. Jesus would go away, but he would send us the Spirit to plead for us when we were accused. We can imagine ourselves on trial before God and in serious risk of being condemned, both for what we have done and for what we have failed to do with our lives. In what way does the Holy Spirit plead on our behalf?

St Paul says it is the Spirit who enables us to cry out to God as our very own Father. I stand trial as a sinful human being, but my Advocate encourages me to plead, 'Abba! Father!', which puts the situation in a completely different light. God cannot resist forgiving his own children. The promises of Isaiah and other prophets are fulfilled: in God's eyes I am not forsaken but chosen, not abandoned but God's delight.

If 'Abba!' is one password, 'Jesus, remember me' is another. The one we call the Good Thief had no case at all to offer to the judge, nothing but a string of offences of theft. He could not promise to improve his record in future, because he had no future. Surely inspired by the Spirit, he did not judge Jesus for not doing enough to help, but took the King at his own word and asked to be included: 'Jesus, remember me when you come into your kingdom.' And that was enough. Completely acquitted.

I am stressing the Good News. People who hear me praise the Good Thief sometimes murmur, 'But what about the other thief?' I presume the other thief also entered the kingdom by the mercy of God, but, unlike the Good Thief, the other thief does not inspire us in any way. The Good Thief is a gift.

28

Unbreakable

The prophets Isaiah, Jeremiah and Ezekiel all spoke of a new and eternal or everlasting covenant which was to come. Jesus, in his words at the Last Supper, is announcing the new covenant in his blood, and the gospel writers clearly identify the two covenants. Jesus' new covenant is the eternal one that was prophesied.

The old-style covenant, whose format I have compared to a hosepipe held upright in the shape of a doorway (up, across and down), was breakable, since it depended too much on human effort. Human beings could not reach up continuously to where God was willing to reach down, so the relationship was always bound to fail sooner or later. Jesus' covenant, however, coming down as it does from heaven in the first instance, can never fail. No matter how badly we perform, God has said we are his first-generation children, and this is the truth for ever. God who is ever the same is not going to break the link, and we cannot break it. Human beings could break the old covenant by not keeping the rules. Our breaking the rules does not break the new covenant, because we are still God's children when we break the rules. We are still God's children even when we do not behave like God's children. The link is always there.

Why does the blood of Jesus belong right there in the creation of the new covenant? I would say it is because to offer his life-blood for us, his sisters and brothers, showed how God's love is given for all time. To say, 'I still love you even though you crucify me' is to say, 'Once I am dead, you cannot change my mind, can you? I love you utterly and completely, and I am the image of my Father and yours.'

29

Unshakeable

God the First Person of the Trinity is the rock which is not built on any other rock, just as God the First Person is the light that nobody else lit, and the love that nobody else loved first. God is the still point at the centre of all reality, physical or spiritual. Everything and everyone else can be moved, but God is always the same, unshakeable.

When Jesus tells us to build our house on a rock, and that the rock in question is his own Way, he is still referring back to his Father as the ultimate rock. The Way of Jesus is to call God 'Abba' and to call Jesus himself 'brother', and to use those two poles to stabilise our lives. If we rely on anyone or anything else, they will all let us down in the end.

For human beings, old age and death are the final teachers, since everything we may have leaned on will have to be left behind. In time we lose parents, spouses, children, brothers, sisters, friends, jobs and careers, talents, sexual joy and every kind of human joy, human ambitions, homes, scenery, money, health, fitness . . . all of these and anything else that we might depend on, they will all either leave us, or else in the end we will have to leave them. If I have built up my self-image entirely upon these, then the wrench will be devastating when we have to go through the door of dying all on our own.

But the things Jesus offers need never be taken away: God's constant love for me as his child no matter how poor my performance, and Jesus' will to take me with him to Paradise if I will only let him. In the security of that rock I can here and now set out to love God back as well as I can, free from false values.

30

The Stronger One

In old litanies calling on Jesus according to his many titles, one of the titles was 'The Stronger One'. This comes first of all from John the Baptist's words of preparation for the coming of Christ, that one 'stronger than I' was coming, who would baptise with the Holy Spirit. Then there is Jesus' own parable or illustration, when he says that if a strong man comes and binds us up then makes free with our house, there we stay unless a stronger one comes and binds up the villain.

The strength of Jesus the Stronger One is used to create freedom for the former victim of the strong one. Jesus can set us free, and nobody or nothing can stand in his way. Even the final enemy Death is no match for him. The enemies of Jesus thought they could silence him for ever and stop the movement and direction of the Holy Spirit by killing Jesus. But all that happened was that Jesus carried on, transfigured and more powerful than ever. The love of God is such that if we deny it, the love becomes even more visible than before.

In ordinary life, Jesus in his greater strength can set us free from countless obstacles and entanglements. By his news that we are first-generation children of God he can set us free from anxiety, from scruples (have I got everything perfect?), from the need to pretend, from the need for success (spiritual or temporal), from despair, from dithering, from slavery to rules and regulations, from being ruled by what people might think of me, from having to fix and judge other people who are not my responsibility, from fear of judgement, from regrets, from the spirit of competition, from needing praise all the time, and even from sin, in the sense that my sins need no longer paralyse me.

31

Divine Jesus

The purpose of this page is to make a simple deduction and then to strengthen it by further reflections. The simple deduction is this: Jesus is divine, Son of God from all eternity into all eternity; Jesus died on the cross to save me; God does not do futile actions, so therefore Jesus' purpose will succeed.

How is it that each of us can say, 'Jesus died for me'? Something unruly, even in many Christians, keeps muttering, 'I never asked him to die for me. What difference does his death make to me?' Jesus died because he would not let anyone be shut out from God's fatherhood or God's mercy. For Jesus salvation is a family affair, and every single child is as precious as any other. The gospel stories invite the reader or hearer to say, 'If I am a leper, Jesus does not shut me out; if I am blind, he will show me the way; if I am shut out by society for being a foreigner, or a criminal, I am not shut out from his kingdom; if I am exploited because I am a woman, or a child, or a servant, Jesus will treat me as an equal.'

Jesus was persecuted because he refused to make any exceptions, but instead welcomed into his kingdom anyone at all who would accept God's forgiveness and refrain from judging others. This was the truth Jesus stood for, and he made it clear that the same truth holds good for all time. Had it not been for Jesus, no one else would ever have dared to bring that enormous freedom of heart into the world, the freedom which I enjoy today.

Jesus died for everyone; therefore he died for me as much as for anyone else. Conversely, I believe, if he did not die for me, he died for no one.

32

No competition

To people of a nervous disposition, a good by-product of the Good News is that it does away with competition. Friendly competition – competition in fun – is always good, but once the whole personality gets involved in competition it can be poison.

The key factor is that no one son or daughter of God is better than another: they are just different. We are all pieces of the same jigsaw, every one different as is the case in a well-made jigsaw puzzle. To be a princess, the daughter of God – a divine princess as well as a royal princess – is something no amount of human effort could reach to. Similarly with a royal and divine prince. Our elder brother is both king and divine, which is what makes us royal and divine. No sports person or scientist or academic or actor or anyone like that could achieve such heights in their field that they would become divine, yet each of us is given that as a free gift.

Jesus thinks big when speaking of the consequences of acting rightly, comparing how a successful servant might be given charge of a whole city, or five or ten cities. Each of us will be given a whole principality, since we are princes and princesses.

Each of us has a unique relationship with God, such that your heaven is bound to be you-shaped, while mine will be me-shaped. We already possess in God everything that our own heart could ever desire. What it comes down to is this: no one can be you better than you can, and nobody can be me better than I can. The race, if there is one, is against our own self, to do the best we can.

33

The naughty child

When I was an adviser to Catholic schools in the Liverpool Catholic Archdiocese it fell to me to revise and enlarge the Junior religious education syllabus, building on the experience the teachers already had with the previous syllabus. I made sure that the revised version included the following statements, loud and clear:

> God loves the naughty child, and the child who fails, and the good child, now and for ever – because they are God's children and not because they are good children. Hence any child can say, 'Sin cannot catch me – I am free. Failure cannot catch me – I am free. I can try to please God, without always being scared of failing. The enemy is defeated.'

Jesus befriended sinners: the good thief, Zacchaeus, the woman who wiped his feet with her hair, Matthew the apostle, the woman with five ex-husbands, the paralysed man let down through the roof on the stretcher, Mary Magdalene, several tax collectors, and the woman caught committing adultery; and he cared for those whose lives were in a mess, like the cripple at the pool, the woman bent double, Bartimaeus, and dozens of other no-hopers. Besides all that, he did not cut off those who let him down, notably the apostles themselves.

Children need to be helped to transfer the stories about Jesus' friends to their own lives. So often parents can start the career of their child by saying, 'He is a good baby', meaning, 'He does not keep us awake at night', which implies that if he cries at night he is a bad baby. And so it can go on. Jesus could forgive the characters who were hammering nails into his hands and feet, so he is justified in asking us not to label our own children.

34

Seek, and you will find

Jesus teaches confidently that anyone who goes looking for God will find God. This teaching relates to what I mentioned before about a certain early Christian writer: that writer said God is always looking towards us and smiling love and kindness in our direction, and the only problem is the way we turn our backs on God and see darkness and shadows instead. Here now is the Master himself saying to look for God where God is, and we will certainly find God.

Another way of looking at the same truth is what I already said about the hosepipe turned so that it makes a U shape rather than a ∩ shape. God is always pouring love and forgiveness down on me and you, and all we have to do is open our ears and hear that message.

There is another wonderful saying of Jesus to be found in St Mark's gospel, which goes like this: 'If you ask for anything in prayer, believe that you have it already, and it will be yours.' This applies, for instance, to asking for forgiveness: if we ask for forgiveness, believing that we are already forgiven, then we will be given forgiveness. If we ask for God's love, believing that we have it already, then God's love will be ours. The love and forgiveness are there for the asking, and all we have to do is ask.

A friend of mine once told me that when she was lost as a little child, and was taken to the police station while enquiries were made, her father eventually turned up to collect her. She looked at her Daddy and said accusingly, 'Where were you when I was looking for you?' We tend to blame God for getting lost.

35

The character of baptism

Theology, like any other branch of learning, has its technical terms, which often take ordinary words and give them a special meaning. Such in Catholic theology is the word 'character'. There are three sacraments, we understand, which have a 'character', meaning 'the reason why the sacrament cannot be repeated'. Once baptised, always baptised; once confirmed, always confirmed; once a priest, a priest for ever. It is in the nature of these three sacraments.

Taking now just the character of baptism, this involves believing that no matter how wicked a baptised person may become, they will never need to be re-baptised. Once a child of God, always a child of God. My own theology teacher, who was steeped in the writings of the early Christian writers, taught us that the character of baptism means that we each have our own place at the table. God's table is the family table, and we each have our own place there, rather like the place-names for each of the guests at a stylish wedding.

In truth every child born into the world is a first-generation child of God; Christians are the ones who celebrate this as Jesus taught them to. We believe it, we celebrate it, we bring up our children on that understanding, with love and forgiveness as top priority. Or at least we try to. In the alternative ending of Mark's gospel we find the words, 'The one who believes and is baptised will be saved; but the one who does not believe will be condemned.' Nothing said against the one not baptised, only the one who does not believe. Jesus offered the bread of the children to a pagan woman; he saved the paralysed man because of the faith of his friends. Those who do not believe what the Good News offers will have to live with bad news till the day they die and see truth.

36

'All sins are forgiven'

The Letter to the Hebrews (10:18) states that there is no further need of offerings for sin now that all sins have been forgiven through the sacrifice of Christ, and quotes the prophetic words of Jeremiah on the new covenant: 'When those days arrive . . . I will never call their sins to mind.' Those days have arrived, the Letter implies.

This way of speaking could also remind us of Jesus' own way of speaking, when he says 'Son, your sins are forgiven,' or 'Daughter, your sins are forgiven.' They are not son or daughter of Jesus, but of the Father of Jesus, and forgiven for that very reason. Jesus waits to find listeners who can rise to believing they are forgiven, then reassures them that they are justified in so believing.

What about Jesus' telling the apostles that 'whose sins you shall retain, they are retained'? How could this be, if all sins are forgiven? The answer is surely that the apostles can only be given authority to distribute forgiveness in the way Jesus their Teacher did. Jesus forgave everything except unforgivingness. He was only intolerant with the intolerant. If all sins are forgiven, and I decide that *your* sins are not to be forgiven, then I have set up a scene at odds with that of Jesus. Your sins are in fact forgiven, but I have put myself outside that scene, and made myself unforgivable as long as I hold my bitterness.

There was an old English ritual for the sacrament of penance which instructed the priest to begin by asking whether the penitent was willing to forgive everyone else. If the answer was 'No', the penitent was told to go away, and come back only when he or she had tried to forgive all enemies.

37

Reconciliation

One of the changes brought about by the Second Vatican Council was a shift in emphasis in the Sacrament of Penance, away from the stress on 'confession' and on to an emphasis on reconciliation. This is the sacrament I wish to focus on for this page, the Sacrament of Reconciliation.

When Catholics come to this sacrament, they need not think they come to have their sins forgiven, since their sins are already forgiven as far as God is concerned, from the moment they asked God for forgiveness in their own hearts. Otherwise the sacrament would not be a privilege for Catholics, something to recommend their faith to others; it would be an extra burden which everyone else is spared. If I as a Catholic could only get my sins forgiven by going to a priest and admitting out loud everything I had done, whereas my neighbour who is not a Catholic can get his sins forgiven just by opening up his heart secretly to God, then I know which I would prefer.

But if my sins are already forgiven, why then go to this sacrament? The result of going is that I get reassurance. I go to a representative of the Church who in turn represents God on this occasion, and say the things about my life that have been worrying me, sins and faults and omissions. My heart misgives me as I say these things, and I wonder, can God really forgive all this? The priest assures me, yes, I am forgiven. In God's name, yes, I am forgiven. Then I can get up and go away in peace. As Shakespeare says about the poet's skill, the sacrament likewise 'gives to airy nothings a local habitation and a name'. I can pinpoint with absolute certainty the moment when I was forgiven. It works, I have tried it.

38

Before and after time

St Paul tells the Ephesians that they were chosen in Christ before the foundation of the world. Clearly he does not mean just the people of Ephesus, but any Christians anywhere at any time. And if any Christians, then the same must apply to any human being at all who might hear the word of God and take it to heart, with baptism of water or baptism of desire.

There is a sense in which any Christian can say, 'Before Abraham was, I am a child of God, greater than John the Baptist the great prophet', since Jesus said the least in the kingdom is greater than John. The child of God is timeless. Therefore God's love for his chosen ones predates the creation of the world, or indeed the creation of the universe: it is outside time.

In that case the forgiveness of God is outside time as well. Anyone can say, 'As far as God is concerned, I am forgiven before the world was created, before I was conceived, before I was born, when I was born, before I ever sinned, while I sinned, after I sinned, now and for ever.' God's love is not stopped by sin, which means that forgiveness is part of the love, since I cannot guarantee not to sin.

A little prayer at the offertory of the Eucharist goes like this: 'By the mystery of this water and wine may we come to share in the divinity of Christ, who humbled himself to share in our humanity.' Every day Christ re-enacts the miracle of Cana, turning the water of our humanity into his divinity, making us sharers in his divine life. His divine life is older than creation, and will still be there when heaven and earth pass away.

39

Reality is friendly

One of the side-effects of the Good News is that it helps us to believe reality is friendly. Not just that pleasant people are friendly, but that the whole universe is friendly.

Scientists have always worked on that basis. If something is wrong in the world, they look for a solution, being pretty sure there will be one somewhere. All the advances of science and technology and medicine over the centuries have come about because scientists use reason to find reasonable solutions and cures; they knew by instinct where to look for discoveries. Drop something and it will fall; night will follow day; and so on to the finding-out of the most useful and complex things in the macro-cosm and the microcosm.

In the spiritual world the same is true. God the ultimate truth is love, and everlasting love means everlasting forgiveness where human frailty is involved. The ultimate reality is forgiveness, and we ignore that fact at our peril. Jesus gives us the wonderful story of the prodigal son, but it has a sting in its tail. The elder brother of the returned wastrel is jealous, and will not come in to the party celebrating his brother's return. The father of the boy pleads with him to join in the forgiveness. Jesus does not tell us whether the elder brother consents to come in, or not, because the answer to that question lies with each and every one of us. If we refuse to associate with those whom God has forgiven, we will ourselves be the losers. If we refuse to share the blanket forgive-ness of God with those we do not approve of, we are excluding ourselves from the family. Jesus is not following a whim, he is stating the nature of reality. God is truth, and the truth, the whole truth, is forgiveness.

40

We recognise truth

We sometimes talk about recognising the truth; yet, when we use the word 'recognise' we usually mean we have seen whatever-it-is before. In the matter of the Good News, to see it is to recognise it for the truth, and how could we recognise it for the truth unless we had seen it before?

We all come from God, and our human reality comes from the truth. There is a kinship between the way we are and the way God is. When we die we go home to God, not to any strange land. Those who are in touch with their own reality and their own being as creatures (created beings) will have eyes open to receive further truth as it is revealed.

Jesus used the cure of blind persons as a sign of what he was most concerned about, namely that people should recognise his teaching for the truth that it is. His enemies were the really blind, the ones he called blind guides, only good for leading other poor blind folk into the ditch. They thought they were independent; they did not see their need. They did not see their need of forgiveness; they were unable to think of all sins being forgiven; they wanted to think they were sinless, and that the sinful should be condemned.

Jesus cured two kinds of physical blindness. The first was of those who were blind from birth, like the man who became able to see but not understand (mistaking humans for walking trees), then able to understand what was what. The second kind was that of Bartimaeus, who used to be able to see but had lost his sight. We all have something of both kinds of blindness. How could we ever understand God's goodness all at once, even if we have seen it before?

41

The love I mean

The First Letter of John speaks a lot about love, and the writer says, 'This is the love I mean, not our love for God but God's love for us when he sent his Son to be the atonement for our sins.' The Good News is God's love for us, not our love for God. Our love for God is a response to the news, our love is not the news itself. The news is independent of my response to it. My response is voluntary, and a poor response will not destroy the news, will not cancel God's love, and will not put me beyond the reach of God's forgiveness.

John's letters are a bit of a jigsaw when they speak about sin. He says we all sin, and whoever say they are not sinners are deceiving themselves, and are indeed calling God a liar. He says whoever sins has never seen God. He says that anyone begotten by God does not sin. But, he also says, if anyone does sin, we have our advocate with the Father, Jesus Christ the sacrifice who takes away our sins and the sins of all the world. How to piece all that together?

We are all sinners, but if we admit that we are all sinners and in need of saving from our sins, then we have Jesus. Jesus was sent to us by his Father out of sheer love, to tell us we are first-generation children of God and therefore guaranteed forgiveness when we need it. Our own experience tells us that however much we regret our weakness, we do carry on sinning in many ways even when we know we are children of God. We do not behave in a manner worthy of our origin. But the fact that we know we are children of God and instantly forgiven enables us to be free from sin. 'The enemy is defeated,' as I used to tell the children and their teachers. We may be wounded, but we can carry on as wounded children, not despair as failed slaves.

42

'My favour rests on you'

'You are my Son, the Beloved; my favour rests on you.' Such is one of the ways of translating the Good News from God at Jesus' baptism. I have said that each of us can take those words to ourselves, by the invitation of Jesus, and say to God, 'I am your beloved son' or 'I am your beloved daughter; your favour rests on me.' How to square that with the saying of both Peter (to Cornelius and family) and Paul (to the Romans) that God has no favourites? Both apostles are using Old Testament words, where it is said that God cannot be bribed, but now seeing a totally new meaning. Now they see that God does not favour the Jewish race above the pagans, but simply chose the Jews to be the much-loved channels to bring the news to the whole beloved human race.

What happens when we take the statement at a personal level, and say that God has no favourites? At first that sounds disappointing, since each of us in our heart of hearts feels like God's favourite person. But if we follow the logic through, the fact that God has no favourites means that God does not favour anybody ahead of me. God the Father loves me, therefore, (and any human being can say this with truth) as much as he loves any other first-generation child of God. As much as Peter or Paul, as much as Mother Teresa or Padre Pio, as much as John of the Cross or Teresa or Thérèse, as much as the Prime Minister or the President, as much as anybody I am secretly jealous of. God loves me as much as he loves his own Son Jesus, since he did not hold back his own Son when it came to saving me. God did not say, 'No, my Son is too precious to put at risk for such as you.' So what it comes to is this: that God's favour does rest on each and every one of us as surely as it does on Jesus himself.

43

With God, no might-have-beens

In the type of philosophy I studied, there was a branch called Natural Theology, which was a study of what might be known about God by reason alone, apart from using scripture and Christian tradition. The most useful item I picked up from this natural theology was 'With God there are no might-have-beens.' It fits in very well with the Good News.

The reasons in philosophy for saying this I cannot now well remember, except that I found it all very convincing. I think the argument ran, that there were so many options as to what might have happened had people done something different, that the whole idea was logically impossible – therefore not even God could go along with it. There were several billions of persons present yesterday in the world, and they all have free will, and there were twenty-four hours of sixty minutes of sixty seconds for each of those people to choose to do something different from what they in fact did. And that was just one day in history. If my father had gone some other place on the day he first met my mother, I might not have been at all. But I am.

The relief of thinking this way fits in very well with the Good News. God is not sitting there at his desk with the blueprint of my life spread out in front of him, saying, 'Tut! Tut!' because I have spoiled the Plan. God starts now, always now. I am here, so God must be here, because I cannot exist without God. Yesterday is forgiven, and regrets over might-have-beens only get in the way. Yesterday is something to learn from, not to grieve over. All will be well. God brings good out of evil: I smash his beautiful stained-glass window, and God quietly and without fuss starts to put it together again in a new pattern.

44

Our God, a Trinity of love

Our God is not a lonely God, but a God of happy endings. From always, God the First Person has been the light that nobody lit, the rock based on no other rock, the love that nobody loved-into-existence.

The Second Person is love-in-return-for-love. Some of the ancient philosophers before Christ arrived at the notion that there must be One who was the origin of truth, of beauty, of justice and of all good. But they did not go on to look at realities like praise, admiration, gratitude, wonder, reliance, trust, in order to find the ultimate origin of those. One person cannot really be the origin of both love and of gratitude for love, of both beauty and of admiration of beauty, without being insufferably vain. Which is easy to see and to say once we know God is a Trinity, and that the one who is wonderful and the one who wonders are two different persons.

The Holy Spirit is the two-way love between the other two divine Persons. The clues are there in the story of the prodigal son. The father loves the son so much that he lets him go and make mistakes, just hoping against hope that he will return some day. From the father's side, a love with no strings. From the son's side comes a love that eventually takes the risk of coming home and trusts that the father's love is still there. Risks on both sides . . . but a happy ending.

When we transfer that to the Trinity, the Father loves the Son with no demands; the Son loves in return, freely. Jesus on the cross was undoubtedly taking a risk, that his Father still loved him. But the risk was well worth taking. Christians believe that when anyone gives unselfish love, it will at last return.

45

Grace comes *gratis*

Our English word 'grace' comes from the Latin word for the same reality, *gratia*, which in turn is kin to the Latin tag we still sometimes use, namely *gratis*, meaning 'free, costing nothing'.

When I was first introduced to the notion of grace, at the tender age of six, the picture I had of it was of something like milk. It had to be liquid, because it got poured into our souls, and you can normally only pour something liquid. It needed to be milk rather than water, because it was to do with making my soul white. That image of grace lurked in the back of my consciousness probably until I studied theology and discovered that grace is a relationship.

There is a fundamental parent/child relationship with God which is established at baptism. It was understood that for those who do not know the value of baptism there is always 'baptism of desire', or in the case of babies the desire of their human parents. That was what was meant by the phrase 'sanctifying grace'. 'Actual grace', then, was any kind of strengthening of that one-to-one relationship, such as comes about, for instance, through the other sacraments.

My point now is that grace comes free. As an adviser I have on occasion tried to persuade teachers to trust in the Good News, only to find them sliding into bad news by means of their wrong notion of grace. They would argue, 'Oh yes, but now we have the sacraments. They are the channels of grace. Our children *have* to use them or else they will never get to heaven. These are the means to get us to heaven.' And thus they were back with the heretic Pelagius, teaching that it is *our* use of the sacraments that saves us, not God's mercy.

46

Jesus the Good Samaritan

In the years before 1966 the gospel of the Good Samaritan was always read on the Sunday when the 'collect' prayer for the day referred to Jesus as the one who raised up our fallen world. That eventually gave me the clue to a new way of looking at the parable: imagine Jesus as the Samaritan and myself as the one who fell among thieves.

I have certainly taken quite a few serious falls on my spiritual journey through life (from Jerusalem to Jericho, as it were). Dangers often lurk in dark places where I can be ambushed, even now. Every time this has happened, I have been rescued. Other human beings have been unable to reach my wounds on these occasions, in the sense that they were as unable to help as the priest and the Levite who passed by on the other side. Jesus on the other hand comes from heaven, from a distant land much further than Samaria.

I had no right to expect or demand that Jesus should help me, but he did. He stopped, he poured wine and oil into my wounds which reached me exactly where I was wounded. He took me on each occasion to some inn where I was looked after, by himself initially; and the debt to him he brushed aside, not only for the past but also for the time until he will come back again.

This story is true not only for me but for anyone who has found Jesus helping them. The story looked at in this way will apply to most Christians in one way or another. And if I look at my Good Samaritan as he leaves me for a time and say, 'How can I ever repay you?', only then will he say, 'If you want to thank me, then when you are better, go and do likewise to someone else.'

47

Even the unforgivable

Jesus himself says that all sins can be forgiven . . . except the sin against the Holy Spirit, which can never be forgiven. He is facing his enemies at the time, who are accusing him of doing his works of healing by the power of the evil spirit.

Later on, Jesus in Jerusalem will ask those same enemies where John the Baptist's authority came from, from heaven or from earth? The proud enemies had failed to turn up at John's baptism except to observe from a distance; they were unwilling to admit they were sinners in need of forgiveness. They would get to heaven by observing all the rules, by their own strength. They were pushing up against the love of God coming down; they were breathing out before they had ever breathed in. On the 'hosepipe' image, they were trying to present God with reasons to honour them, rather than letting God do the honours.

So their sin, and the sin of anyone else who thinks that way, is not able to be forgiven, because not even God can successfully forgive another who does not want to be forgiven. But when Jesus says this sin can never be forgiven, he must surely mean 'can never be forgiven as long as the sinner persists in it'. All the proud person has to do is turn round, admit weakness, let God love and forgive, turn and go with the stream of the Holy Spirit instead of resisting it.

When the enemies of Jesus taunted him on the cross and said, 'He saved others; he cannot save himself', I think they spoke the truth. It is in the nature of every person, even the Second Person of the Trinity, that we need to be loved first by God the First Person. Once we see that clearly, then we can save others.

48

Mark: healing comes first

The gospel of Mark is the earliest gospel to be completed. We could almost say that Mark invented the literary form of 'gospel', which means Good News. What I wish to point out here is that in the first half of the whole book of sixteen chapters there are no demands except to let ourselves be healed, fed and forgiven. The second half of the book of Mark is about Jesus' suffering and death and resurrection, outlining Jesus' response to his Father and our possible response to Jesus, but all of that comes second. The love comes down before it finds its way back to God again.

If Jesus had come simply as a healer of physical illness in this life, he was not very successful. A few hundred healed in his earthly lifetime, a few more in each generation after that, but most of us left exactly where we were before, except for the advances in medicine. No, the cures Jesus performed were signs, signs of what the Good News can do and does for all generations.

Because I am a child of God I need not stay, as it were, on my stretcher, paralysed by my past failures: my sins are forgiven, so I can get up right away and go on my way home. I am not a leper, but as a child of God I am as good as anyone else. I am not unclean or untouchable, since I am of royal and divine blood. I need not be prey to a thousand warring anxieties within me, since for Jesus there is only one thing necessary: drown all the anxieties in the waters of God's forgiveness and then ask Jesus what he wants me to do.

Even death is only a sleep, from which we will awake to find Jesus holding our hand and calling us, while our loved ones look on.

49

Mark: feeding comes next

After the healing comes the feeding. At the end of the healing stories in the first five chapters of Mark came the little girl brought back to life. She was hungry, so Jesus told her parents to give her something to eat. In the meantime the people following Jesus around, and Jesus himself, had less and less space for eating or for anything else, there were so many in the crowds. Jesus himself is no longer welcome in the synagogues, so he goes out on to a hillside and looks after the crowds there.

Unlike the situation in the synagogues, where at that time sinners were not welcome and the sick were suspect, out on the hillside with Jesus there were no conditions of acceptance. If you wanted to come, you just turned up. You did not have to prove that you were worthy to be there. If you could not see, you got someone to take you; if you were crippled, you got someone to carry you. Jesus showed compassion, because they were like sheep without a shepherd. He fed them, and although it should have cost two hundred days' wages, there was no charge. The grass was green, for them to sit down on. There was plenty of bread over, and a lakeful of water: no one got left out.

All of this fits in, as one would expect, with the shape of the action of the Holy Spirit. The first movement of the symphony is God's compassion and care for each and every one of his children; the second movement is the willingness of the children to be called children and treated as children. They bring their ills for healing, then they find there is a gap in their lives where the illness used to be, so they are hungry, and they look to God to feed them. They do not need to fill the gap by their own money or resources.

50

Mark: then comes recognition

Along with the healing and particularly the feeding stories in Mark's gospel there is another theme drawing towards a climax, namely recognition. Jesus is exasperated because his own chosen disciples cannot recognise who he is, in spite of his enormous sign of the Shepherd who has compassion and makes the sheep lie down on the green grass beside the waters, and feeds them with a feast that costs them nothing, a feast from which nobody at all is excluded, not even his enemies. Another big sign Mark records is the way Jesus fed four thousand in the desert, lest they faint on the way home, since they had come a long way and had been with him days on end. He was the Shepherd God had said would come, and he was the prophet-like-Moses that Moses had said would come, a prophet like Moses who had given them manna from God in their years in the desert long ago. But could the disciples see that? Not they!

They looked and looked but did not see; they listened and listened but did not hear. Jesus gave the sign of curing the blind man who first could not see, then could not understand what he saw. Besides, Jesus healed the man deaf from birth, who could make noises but not make sense with his noises. Finally with Peter the penny dropped: 'You are the Christ.'

At this stage the only person to tell about it is God, to thank God. Peter is told to be quiet; the deaf one cured and the blind one cured likewise, told to be quiet about it. For us today as readers and hearers of the gospel, the requirement at this stage in Mark is simply to acknowledge what way the Holy Spirit travels. Can we, do we dare to, believe Jesus when he says that God does the healing and saving of us; we cannot do it ourselves?

51

Mark: way of the cross

How can the way of the cross ever be Good News? Yet the second half of Mark's gospel is largely to do with the way of the cross. No sooner has Peter recognised Jesus as the Christ, the Messiah, bringing the Good News, than Peter trips over a stumbling block. Jesus starts to talk about going to Jerusalem and being sure to be crucified, and Peter cannot square that with his idea of what the Christ is all about. Surely, Peter implies, everyone will recognise Jesus as he has done, and all will start to love and forgive one another? Jesus says, not so; it will not be as easy as that.

There and then Jesus invites all those who wish to be followers of his to take up their cross and follow him. The visual example given later in the gospel is that of Simon of Cyrene, the man who was forced by the soldiers to carry the cross through the streets of Jerusalem with Jesus.

But notice: Jesus says, 'Whoever wants to be a follower of mine . . .' He does not say, 'Whoever wants to be saved by me must take up the cross.' In gospel language followers are those who give their whole lives to Jesus. There will be multitudes more people saved than there ever will be followers of Jesus. Jesus has already healed and fed crowds of people without making any demands on them. There were five thousand and more people fed on the hillside by Jesus, assisted in the distribution by just twelve chosen disciples. The disciples (the chosen ones, the followers) are chosen to help Jesus save the others. Theirs is a privilege: the whole success does not depend on them. We therefore have a genuine choice, as to whether we wish to take up our cross and follow Jesus. We can be saved by Jesus, whether or no, if we ask him.

52

Mark: the chalice

In Mark's gospel Jesus refers to his coming sufferings as 'the cup that I drink'. 'Can you drink the cup that I drink?' he asks James and John, meaning can they cope with having to suffer the way Jesus will have to suffer? There is an obvious connection between the cup of suffering and the cup of the Eucharist which Jesus blesses at the Last Supper, calling it 'my blood of the new covenant'. How can the cup be Good News?

In so far as the chalice means Jesus' sufferings, that is Good News because it is his blood poured out 'for all'. Jesus dying saved me, whether or not I will ever succeed in drinking the same cup myself. He died for the forgiveness of sins; I admit that I am a sinner in need of being put to rights with God; I am happy to know from Jesus that God loves me in spite of my being a sinner.

My own chalice is Good News for two reasons. First of all, the whole scene of the cross, and Jesus being crucified, is clear proof that suffering is not sent by God as a punishment for bad behaviour. There is something in human nature that feels resentful against God when things go badly after we have been doing the best we could. Jesus was sinless and a shining example of goodness, yet he ended up by being executed as a criminal. We are children of God, and we should remember that God was not blaming Jesus his Son for past misdeeds.

The other aspect of Good News in the chalice is that, like the apostles, every Christian who has been healed and fed by Jesus is *invited* to spread the Good News of forgiveness along with Jesus. We start out thinking this will be easy, but, like Peter, James and John, we will learn.

53

Manifesto (Martin Luther)

I could not agree with every word Martin Luther ever wrote, but here is a paragraph or two I can go along with wholeheartedly. They come from one of his Manifestos of 1520, *Concerning Christian Liberty*. The passage I have in mind begins with a reference to the Letter of St Paul to the Philippians, from which Luther deduces that every Christian, though free as a child of God, should have the same mind as Christ Jesus, and put aside that freedom from having to do good works, becoming a servant and a slave to all others. As a forgiven sinner the Christian should reason thus (says Luther):

> For such a Father who has overwhelmed me with these inestimable riches of his, why should I not freely, cheerfully, and with my whole heart and from voluntary zeal, do all that I know will be pleasing in his sight. I will therefore give myself, as a sort of Christ, to my neighbour, as Christ has given himself to me; and will do nothing in this life except what I see will be needful and wholesome for my neighbour, since by faith I would abound in all good things in Christ.
>
> Thus from faith flow forth love and joy in the Lord, and from love a cheerful, willing, free spirit, disposed to serve our neighbour voluntarily, without taking any account of gratitude (from those I serve) or ingratitude, praise or blame, gain or loss.
>
> This is that Christian liberty, our faith, the effect of which is, not that we should be careless or lead a bad life, but that no one should need the law or works for justification or salvation.

54

'We are merely servants'

Jesus has many stories about servants and slaves. He even saw himself as being the Servant prophesied by Isaiah. Some of the servant stories told by Jesus involve rewards for doing well, but there is one story or parable which makes us think twice about whether servants may expect to be rewarded. This is the one in Luke's gospel (17:7-10) about whether the master will make a fuss of the servant when he comes in from working in the fields, saying, 'Draw up a chair, join me at the table for supper.' (I am paraphrasing, of course.) Does not the master say, 'Get my supper and serve it to me, and when I have finished, you can have yours'? Servants should not expect thanks for doing what they were supposed to do. So, too, we as followers of Jesus should not expect thanks from God, but should dub ourselves 'worthless servants' and admit that at best we have only done what we were told to do. That is the line of this particular servant story.

What can we deduce from this? The prodigal son coming home had his head filled with the notion of being a servant, and paying his way. Jesus would say this is not the point: his parable does not allow the son to make the request but shows him cut off, before he could make it, by the father's generous welcome.

We are welcomed home to God because we are children of God and loved as such. Our service to God is what we do freely in gratitude for God's love given and promised for ever. We cannot expect the giver to be grateful for our gratitude. If we expect thanks for saying 'Thank you' we are likely to be disappointed. We would be unwise to limit God's love that way.

55

Good News in Paul (I)

St Paul is the one who brought the phrase 'justified by faith' into the Christian vocabulary. He did not invent the reality itself, which comes from Jesus, but he did use those three words from the Old Testament to apply to Jesus' teaching. What the words mean is this: You or I turn up in heaven, and someone of a Pharisee turn of mind challenges us: 'How dare you go in there? You have not kept God's laws perfectly as I have. How can you justify your presence?' And we reply, 'I believed, on the strength of Jesus, that God is my *Abba*, my own Father. And I have found it to be as Jesus told me. I know well my own faults, but my Father has welcomed me.'

This was not the way Paul himself was brought up to believe. He was a Pharisee and a very dedicated one, persecuting the followers of Jesus to the limit of his ability. What changed Paul was his vision on the road to Damascus. This Jesus, whom he believed dead, appeared to him and spoke to him. The vision was from God; it could only have been from God. Paul himself became a follower of Jesus, and for the rest of his life he never wavered, his faith never even flickered.

When Paul speaks about faith, he often says that what saves us is faith in Jesus Christ the Lord. At first sight that seems to be rather meaningless. But Paul is saying that he believes Jesus is the Messiah, the one chosen before time by God to bring us the truth. He is saying that Jesus is the Lord, the Son of God, still very much alive and never to die again, and that therefore his teachings are true and should be trusted. The *Abba* of Jesus is our *Abba*. The stories of the lost sheep, the lost coin and the lost boy apply to us.

56

Good News in Paul (II)

Paul was brought up from childhood to believe that what mattered most in all the world was to keep the Jewish laws perfectly, out of reverence for the one true God. The desire to keep all the laws perfectly is very praiseworthy, but the only trouble is that many of the Jews themselves could not manage the task, to say nothing of the countless millions, of other faiths, whom the Jews might have hoped would eventually come round to their way of thinking. There had been for centuries a hope that Jerusalem would become the centre of the believing world, and all nations would serve the one true God in the Jewish manner.

For Paul it was a tremendous change of mind to see anything other than the Law as the means of salvation. For Paul to take to heart the story of the prodigal son and the teaching implied in that story, that must have been a shock. It was less of a shock to Paul, since he had suddenly seen the point and could never again rely on the Law; it was more of a shock to his fellow Pharisees and to the early Christians, because they found it hard to believe Paul really meant what he was now teaching.

We tend to forget that the Law included the Ten Commandments. Paul now sees that keeping the Ten Commandments is not the way to heaven. Even my teachers in primary school would have been shocked to know that! Of course behaviour matters, and any Christian will want to take on board the Ten Commandments and keep them. But they are not the most important thing. The most important thing is belief and trust in Jesus our Saviour. Trusting Jesus did not make Paul slack in doing good works, and nor did it make Zacchaeus slack. Neither will it make any other Christian slack in goodness.

.

57

One great commandment

For a Christian there is only one great commandment, not two. When Jesus was asked which was the greatest of the commandments and he replied with one and then added another, he was talking about the greatest commandments *of the Law*. Matthew's gospel says so, quite explicitly. These were the two greatest commandments so far, but not the greatest ever to be. But Jesus did not come simply to agree with what had been taught so far; he came to perfect it. I think we as Christians do Jesus a disservice if we take those two commandments as being his own two great commandments. If that was all there was to it, why did he have to come and die on a cross? We had those two already. Luke's gospel even makes the questioner be the one who comes up with the answer, so who needed Jesus?

The two great commandments of the Law said, 'Love God with all your heart; and love your neighbour as yourself'. Jesus' one great commandment is 'Love one another as I have loved you', which is radically different. The two from the Law start here, on the ground. By my own strength I am to love God one hundred per cent, and my neighbour as much as I love myself, two things I dearly wish to do but two things I am quite incapable of doing for any length of time. This is a case of the hosepipe in the ∩ shape, to use my earlier analogy.

Jesus' one commandment is of the other shape, namely U. I am to love my neighbour the way Jesus loved me. How did Jesus love me? Without strings, even when he was being crucified. I am to look and see and believe how much God loves me, namely freely. Then love and forgive all others likewise. Jesus' one commandment incorporates the Good News.

58

'My burden is light'

Jesus' one great commandment is light, because it is able to be kept. So long as we keep our eyes fixed on the love Jesus had and has for us, then we know our poor efforts in return will be accepted. Our failings are already forgiven as we fail, so we have no need to lose heart. We are given eagles' wings, we need never tire; they are eagles' wings provided by Jesus and his new covenant, although they were promised from the days of the old covenant.

Jesus says his burden is light. How can the carrying of the cross be light? Well, to start with, the carrying of the cross is voluntary, as I have already pointed out. Nobody has to be a dedicated disciple of Jesus in order to be saved by Jesus. But if we wish to love him in return, as we normally will, once we know how well he has loved us, then there is no pass mark that we have to reach in some examination or test. We simply do our best, not looking back at our own failures but pressing on with today and tomorrow. That is what eased the burden for me personally once I learned the Good News: the pressure of keeping up and having to get everything right had been a great load until then.

Another aspect of Jesus saying that his burden is light is this: if I have a heavy burden which I could drop, then why don't I? Evidently it is not from Jesus. Any self-imposed burden may be dropped once it becomes too heavy. If I begin to find the writing of this little book too wearisome, I can drop it in the knowledge that it is no longer Jesus' wish. But Jesus yoked to me will help me to carry any heavy burdens which I cannot drop, like unavoidable sickness. It is not his burden, but he helps me carry mine.

59

Forgiving is a joy

We tend to think of forgiving as a burden, something difficult we have to do. In fact, once we try it with our whole heart, it is a joy. If we only stop and think about the matter, it is judging other people and keeping them straight that is the burden. To forgive is to find myself forgiven. On this subject I do not think I can do better than quote what I wrote in 1977 in a book long out of print.

The day we forgive everyone else, that day the sun shines new, and all the stars dance in heaven. The very air is different. God loves me. I am God's beloved child. God will never remove his love from me. No matter what I have done, no matter what I do in the future, God's love for me is settled.

You may despise me, you may say quite rightly that I am lazy and selfish, that I have not strained myself for you or for the unhappy and unfortunate of the world. I know that. But God has forgiven me, so your blame cannot reach me. God is the one who has eternal life, and God says I will do to take along. God accepts me. He is the one I answer to, not you.

By the same token, I do not expect you to answer to me for what you do, or for what you fail to do. I am not appointed to be your judge. I hereby resign from the Bench.

The day we forgive everyone else, that day we enter the kingdom of heaven. We step into a 'forgiven world' where there is no longer a sword of Damocles hanging over our head. I believe in the forgiveness of sins, as the Apostles' Creed bids me, your sins as well as mine.

60

Forgive yourself

Each of us may rightly say to ourselves, 'God has forgiven you. You have the very best precedent therefore for forgiving yourself.' Why should we think we know better than God? The difficulty is partly one of temperament. Some people are able easily to shake off what happened yesterday; others tend to brood.

Almost certainly, the brooding comes from a kind of inverted pride. Why, in the wheeling of the stars, should what I did *not quite perfectly* yesterday matter so much that it makes me sad today? I am not really as important as all that.

This is a perfect example of what lies behind the story of Jesus where he liberates the paralysed man, the one let down through the roof on a stretcher. People who let their faults or failings of yesterday get in the way of doing their best today are paralysed. Jesus' answer is 'Son', or, as the case may be, 'Daughter, your sins are forgiven. Get up now and go home to your true self.'

The ultimate danger of not forgiving ourselves is that we might be tempted to commit suicide. Whereas Peter was humble enough to let himself be forgiven, Judas seemingly was not. Nowadays the Christian Church is less judgemental about suicide than it used to be, and that is a good thing: Judas was forgiven by Jesus even as he gave the traitor's kiss, and I am quite sure Jesus did not change his mind afterwards. But the tendency to think our sins so important that they are beyond God's mercy is a disease, and one we should cure in its early stages if at all possible.

61

The two sides of the gospel

It is easy to verify that there are two sides to the gospel as proclaimed by Jesus. In his stories and in his teachings there are sheep and there are shepherds; there are fish and there are fishers; there are coins and there are coin-seekers; the light shines on people and people shine the light; the rock supports people and people become rock-like for others; there are little children and there are powerful people; there are lost people and there are guides; there are sons and daughters and there are servants; there is Mary and there is Martha her sister.

In all of these pairs, the first-mentioned is the necessary prelude as far as human beings are concerned. I am the sheep, lost until gathered into God's flock; I am the fish, nobody's until gathered into God's net. I am the coin, unaware, till I am told, that God's image is on me. I am in the dark until God's light shines on me. I am on shaky foundations until my feet rest on the rock of God's love. I am a little child quite incapable of crossing the dangerous road unless God takes my hand. I cannot even get from Jerusalem to Jericho in one piece unless some Good Samaritan helps me. I am God's child *first*, God's servant only secondarily. I will do all the wrong things like Martha unless I sit down and listen to Jesus as Mary did.

Only when this first stage has been absorbed (whichever way we choose to picture it) are we then invited to become shepherds ourselves, and fishers, and coin-seekers, and light-for-others, and rock-for-others, and guides to help the children across the dangerous road. Only then can we properly become Good Samaritans, good servants, well instructed hosts to the divinity.

62

We still need to ask for forgiveness

One of the things that puts good people off believing the Good News is that they think it rules out the need for forgiveness. Of course it does not. May I quote again the precious saying of Jesus to be found in Mark: 'If you ask for something in prayer, believe that you have it already, and it will be yours' (Mark 11:24). He is saying, we need to ask for forgiveness; he is saying, we need to believe we have it already; then, he says, we will get it.

In our post-Christian world, when so many people, young and old, have opted out of the traditional Christian churches, there is a general feeling among such people that forgiveness is irrelevant. They claim to get on very well without it, at least as far as God is concerned. They are not aware that anything they have done has offended a God they are not sure they believe in anyway. They carry on regardless, neither forgiven nor unforgiven.

Such a state of mind is not what the Good News is all about. They are forgiven, as far as God is concerned, just as we all are. But they have to live with their mistakes as these accumulate, because they have no basic truth in their minds and hearts that can free them from the past and the future. It is one thing to have decided that the regulations of any one Christian church are not the only way to a perfect life, and that God can bypass his own rules if he chooses to; it is another thing to miss the one thing that matters: forgiveness.

Just because we are not short of air to breathe, that does not mean we do not need air. Of course we do. Just because forgiveness is there for the asking, that does not mean we do not need it. Of course we do.

63

After Bishop Berkeley

This page holds ideas I got from reading about the theories of Bishop Berkeley, philosopher, Bishop of Cloyne in Ireland from 1734 to 1753. I doubt whether he would agree with my ideas, but I got them from reading his.

Each human being can say this: 'As I look out through my eyes, I see a scene that nobody else in the whole world sees but me. Even if you, neighbour, stand beside me, you see me on your left, I see you on my right, and we have a slightly different angle on what lies before us.' Those who believe in God can add, 'Nobody else at all sees exactly what I see, except me . . . and God.'

It is the same with hearing: nobody else hears what I hear exactly as I hear it, but I do not have to tell God what it sounds like. I would say the case is the same with feelings: nobody else knows exactly what I am feeling, except me and God. I can describe my vision, what I hear, what I feel to another person, but only God knows it direct.

Bishop Berkeley in his writings stressed the separateness of the reality of what each of us sees, hears and feels. There is a real world out there (I would say), but each human being has a separate window on that world, from a room which is itself underpinned by God. My feelings are real, and all reality is underpinned by God or it could not exist. It is as if the whole universe is created all over again for each one of us: the same universe, but from a different point of view. I usually compare the way four players can enjoy the same game of Ludo. All this may sound exotic, but it is only a logical conclusion from the way my mother taught me to share my thoughts with God.

64

Why is mine a plank?

Why is mine a plank, and yours only a speck of dust? This was always the thought I had after hearing Jesus' remark about removing the plank from my own eye before attempting to remove the speck from my neighbour's eye. Much the same thought used to come to me on hearing the story of the man who was let off the debt of ten thousand talents, but who got into trouble again for not letting his debtor off a debt of a hundred denarii. A denarius was a day's wages; one talent was about the same as fifteen years' wages for a labourer. Jesus expects me to identify with the man in the middle, so why is my debt so enormously greater than the other person's?

I would find the answer in what I have just been saying about Bishop Berkeley. God has given to me personally the whole inner world of my sight, my hearing, my mind, my memory, and along with that the whole universe and anything else there may turn out to be beyond or besides the whole universe. The whole universe is mine, from my point of view, and nobody else can have it from that particular point of view of mine. 'All I have is yours,' says the father to the elder brother in Jesus' parable of the lost son. 'All things are yours,' says St Paul, including for good measure life and death and the present and the future. It all adds up to a fair-sized plank compared to the little speck of a grievance I have with my neighbour. It is on a grand scale, compared to my grudge over the small debt I am intent on reclaiming from someone else.

The joy of Jesus' teaching is that if I can only take my mind off my grudges, then I will see that in truth everything is mine, and mine in a way that nobody else can take away from me.

65

God is simple

God is simple. This is a technical term in Catholic philosophy and theology, meaning that wherever God is, the whole of God is. God is single-fold, God cannot be divided up into parts.

The great consolation of that for human beings is that they can say, 'I have the whole of God's attention, all the time.' If God is behind my eyes, looking out with me and sharing the scene, how intimate that makes our union! If I raise my eyes above the head of the person I am speaking to, and look at the pictures on the wall beyond, God and I know what picture, and what feature of what picture, I am looking at. Nobody else does. And this in spite of the fact that the same God is the force behind the whole universe of stars.

God is simple even though God is Trinity. I can with truth look out at my world and say, 'Father, only you and I can see this scene. We can see Christ everywhere, and your Spirit goes out to him everywhere in love.' Or else I can look out and say, 'Jesus, nobody knows the trouble I feel except you. Help me to see God everywhere and in all things. Share with me your trusting love-in-return for the Father who will make all well.'

God knows all my thoughts as I think them, and shares my memories with me. We experienced together the events that I now call to mind, and now we remember them together.

Every tiny atom in the universe has the simple presence of God as we do, but we human beings have the enormous privilege of awareness.

66

The veil torn, seven freedoms

When Jesus died, the gospels relate that the veil of the temple was torn in two, from top to bottom. That statement is not just there for dramatic effect, it has a lot of meaning. If anyone from Britain had wanted to get as close as possible to the God of Abraham, Isaac and Jacob in the days before Jesus, they would have had to travel by sail, or by sea and land, to find the Holy Land. Once there they would have had to find their way to Jerusalem, the holy city. Then they would have had to ask the way to the temple, unless perhaps they could already see it towering above other buildings. Then they would have had to walk across the court of the Gentiles. From then on they could have got no further, unless they were Jews themselves. The next court admitted Jewish women, but that was as far as even a Jewish woman could get. Then a court where Jewish men could go, but they could not enter the Holy Place which was within that court unless they were priests. As for the Holy of Holies, only the high priest or a delegate could enter through that final veil.

That veil was the one torn down by the death of Jesus. Along with that barrier, all the other barriers disappeared at the same time. Nowadays people from anywhere do not have to leave our own shores to find God; we do not have to go to the Holy Land or any other land to find God; we do not have to go to a particular building to find God; although a Gentile, I am no longer held up at the limit of the court of the Gentiles; women or men, there is no bar on either of us; I do not have to be a priest; I do not have to be the high priest, or delegated by him. Like a little child, the son or daughter of God, we can go in without even knocking to the God always lovingly present in our own awareness. The temple has come home to each of us.

67

Friends do not cause
needless pain on purpose

At some time or another we all come across the problem Peter met with and did not cope with. We believe Jesus is the Christ and that he brings the truth. We believe him when he tells us that God is our Father and that is why God loves us. But then we stumble. Why does a loving God let us suffer horrible things? Why did Jesus have to face the cross? Why are there still wars, and rumours of wars, and earthquakes, and cyclones, and tidal waves? And why do so many of our beloved friends die untimely deaths from cancer?

Jesus made it quite clear that in spite of his being who he was, there would still be suffering in this world. What am I to say when suffering hits me personally? Supposing I am the one who is found to have cancer? Well, God is love, God loves me personally. God is my friend. Any friend of mine does not cause me needless pain on purpose, or else that is no friend of mine.

I could no longer call anyone my friend if they were to cause me deep pain on purpose when there was no need for it in the first place. Friends often cause us pain without meaning to, and they remain friends. But to cause needless pain with both eyes open, that is usually enough to break a human friendship.

God is my friend. God does not do needless things. God does not cause needless pain on purpose. When I pray for pain to be removed and it does not go, then I know it cannot be removed right away, or otherwise God my friend would remove it. Even Jesus did not have his request about his chalice answered right away. He had to wait and to trust.

68

No taxes for the children

There is a strange little story in St Matthew's gospel which some people find off-putting. The story ends up with Jesus telling Peter to go fishing, and the first fish he catches will have a coin in its mouth, just enough to pay the temple tax for the two of them.

It would be a pity to dismiss the story as a stray from *The Arabian Nights*, because it contains a very consoling truth about the Good News. We are children of God, and therefore we do not owe God any taxes.

The collectors of the temple tax came to Peter, wanting to know if Jesus paid the temple tax or not. Peter was unsure of the answer, so he went and asked Jesus. Jesus replied with a question, 'Who do earthly kings exact taxes from, their own children, or the rest of the population?' Peter guessed it was not from their children, only from the others. Well and good, says Jesus: in effect, you and I, Peter, are both children of the King whose palace (the temple) is to be paid for by taxes. So the others have a duty to pay the taxes, not us. However – and here Jesus is speaking as the divine Son who empties himself and becomes like a servant – Peter should pay up for them both. God would provide. So he sends Peter off fishing for the wherewithal. We are all of us children of God, but we take on service as a voluntary 'Thank you' to God.

The story, incidentally, does not say that Peter actually found the coin in the mouth of the fish. Maybe Peter just had to keep on fishing until he had two drachmas' worth of a catch. Who knows?

69

Not Hagar's children

In the fourth chapter of Paul's Letter to the Galatians he gives us an allegory. We are, as it were, the children of Sarah, wife of Abraham, not children of Hagar the slave whose children were also fathered by Abraham. As children born into the new covenant we are free by birth, not slaves along with a mother still needing to be set free. In the ancient world, children born to a free woman were free as well, but children born to a slave were slaves.

I have listed already some of the things our status as free-born gives us. We are now not slaves to anxiety, to scruples; if we have not completed our allotted tasks we do not need to pretend that we have. We have no desperate need to succeed in our career or in our marriage or in any other vocation; we do not have to be wonderful at praying or good works in any way that must reach a certain standard. We need not despair if we turn out to be total failures. We need not spend ages dithering as to how to please God our employer: we just do the best we can.

We are even exempt from prosecution if we have done wrong: all we have to do is apologise and try to do better next time. We are not rule-bound, we need not be always looking to see what other people think of us, since the Lord is our Father and loves us unchangeably. We do not have to serve on the Bench or the jury and to judge other people. We are free from regrets, since God who is our life has no regrets in our regard. There is no competition for the master's favour, such as slaves have to endure. We do not need praise, since we have love. Like Jesus, we still take on the duties and tasks of the servant or slave, but we do so freely, as children for whom there are no taxes.

70

The woman at the well

In the fourth chapter of John's gospel we have the beautiful story of Jesus resting beside Jacob's well at Sychar in Samaria, and his long conversation with the woman there who had come to draw water. Eyebrows were raised by the disciples of Jesus when they returned and found him speaking alone with this woman. It could even be that she had come to the well at an unusual time of day because she was not welcome to rub shoulders with the other women of the town.

To me it is an ever-fresh fact that Jesus was quite happy to talk with her on highly spiritual subjects though he knew she had had five husbands and was with a sixth partner now, outside marriage. He did not say, 'You wicked woman!' He did not say, 'You complete failure!' He did not say, 'Go home and find your first husband (or the first in line out of the five that is still alive). Give up your present man and go back to the first; then come back and we will talk.' He did not say, 'Go and get shut of the present man at all costs, then maybe we'll talk about living water.'

As he would later do with Zacchaeus, he treats this woman as being worthy of respect, and she responds in kind. When she begins to comprehend what Jesus is offering, she is thrilled and delighted, and goes off to bring most of the town to listen to Jesus. To begin with, they came to investigate what she was saying to them; but they stayed, and wanted Jesus to stay, because of what he himself was able to give them. The woman became an ambassador of the Good News. And not even at the end of the chapter are we told that Jesus set conditions for her. He does not even say, 'Go, and sin no more.'

71

The Resurrection convergence

If Jesus did not rise from the dead, then there is no Good News. Evil would have triumphed, and we could all end up on a cross for all God cared, and that would be that. Where does the evidence for the Resurrection come from?

It is not a case of a fable that grew and grew in the telling. There are several independent sources of witness to the fact of Jesus' being risen. There is the version of Mark, which is repeated by Matthew and Luke. Then Matthew has his own independent version of what happened, and Luke too has his own version which does not come from Mark. There is the version of John's gospel, and the further version in that gospel which stems from John's disciples.

The evidence from Paul in his First Letter to the Corinthians dates from only three years after the Resurrection itself. He tells the Corinthians that the truth about Jesus' death and Resurrection which he handed to them about AD 48 was like a deposit held in a bank, since Paul himself was taught it fifteen years earlier, neither more nor less than the original message. Perhaps even closer to the events themselves are the speeches of Peter written out in Luke's Acts of the Apostles, speeches which may date from the very year of the Resurrection. They use language and terminology that had gone out of date by the time Luke finally wrote that book. Then, too, there is the fact that Paul can write to churches all over the Mediterranean, knowing that they believe all he believes.

Each of these sources agrees on the basic message, and the apostles were so sure the Resurrection appearances were from God that they were willing to die for the truth of them.

72

More about the Resurrection

What was at the heart of the Resurrection message? The various accounts differ among themselves over some of the details, but they all agree about the basic message: that Christ died, for our sins, according to the scriptures; that he was buried; that he rose, on the third day, according to the scriptures; that he appeared to the Eleven, that he gave a special appearance or a message to Peter, and that he appeared to many together; that women were the first witnesses; that the tomb was empty from early on the Sunday; and that Jesus was recognisably himself, even though difficult to recognise at first.

There has been some puzzlement about where, according to what scriptures, the Messiah could have been expected to rise on the third day. There are several passages that could be seen as prophecies that the Christ would rise again after death, but where does the Old Testament say it would be on the third day? The most plausible answer is that in Psalm 16 the Lord God is shown to say, 'I will not allow my Holy One to see corruption.' When we compare that with the story of Jesus delaying two days, then arriving on the fourth day to raise Lazarus *whose body was already corrupting*, the psalm could be taken by Peter to mean the Christ must rise on the third day. That is why he uses that psalm as a scripture prophecy of Jesus' Resurrection (Acts 2:27-31).

The stress on recognition is consoling, definitely part of the Good News for me. It means we shall recognise our friends and loved ones in heaven, even if with difficulty at first, since Jesus promises the same glory to us as his own. The appearances of Jesus left the disciples absolutely sure they would see him again; it was now quite impossible that the love he had for them was only temporary.

73

Even those who think
themselves unforgivable

There are people who are convinced they can never be forgiven, for what they have done or for what they have failed to do. They are not happy people. Some go so far as to wish they had never been born, because it is such misery to live unforgiven. They dread their own birthday; they pity every little child born into the world.

Clearly these people are not Pharisees. Those of a Pharisee turn of mind do not see any sins except other people's; they themselves are more or less perfect. Those we think of as Pharisees are not asking for forgiveness, either for themselves or for anyone else. What they want is justice only, not realising that in God justice and forgiveness are one and the same. They run the risk of getting exactly what they deserve, and not a penny more.

But those who fear they will never be forgiven are in fact ripe for forgiveness, nothing like the Pharisees. Yet I have spent hours and hours with some of these, trying to persuade them that the Good News applies to them. Sometimes, I am sure, what afflicts them is a disease or a malady, real depression or the down-side of manic-depression, such as only proper medical treatment can cure in this life. They are like people in a wood or a forest who can see only tanglewood in front of them, when I, only twenty yards to the right of them, can see the path clearly.

The main truth is, the path ahead is there. These people may indeed go through hell on earth, but God can turn the mourning into dancing in a very short time, when the time comes. For such as these, all will be well in the end.

74

The beloved disciple

I have a theory about the beloved disciple. The beloved disciple is whoever reads the gospel of John or hears it read. In the history of visions and special moments given to human beings by God, there are some which are for the benefit of the person who receives them, and some which are given to be shared. The vision of Jesus at his baptism was for him and then for all of us: the vision of John, of himself as 'the disciple Jesus loved', is for John first, but then also for all of us.

The one who reclined by Jesus at the last supper, close enough to lean back and talk to Jesus reclining behind him, is 'the one Jesus loved'. According to the language John uses, the Son was 'closest to the Father's heart', and so is the disciple Jesus loves closest to the heart of Jesus. As the Father loves the Son, the Son loves the disciple; as the Son loves the disciple, so can the disciple love the neighbour. Peter had to signal to John to ask a quiet question at the last supper. We disciples can all speak in total privacy to Jesus any time at all.

The beloved disciple receives Mary as mother. The Catholic Church has always believed that that joy was for every disciple, not just John. The beloved disciple sees the tomb empty, and without having seen Jesus still believes that he is risen. The beloved disciple is the first to spot the presence of the risen Jesus when at last he can be seen. The beloved disciple is able to wait for the presence of Jesus to return in visible form, not saying, 'Perhaps he does not love me any more', but 'I know the one he asks to wait is one he loves'. The phrase 'beloved disciple' must mean something that can apply to all, or otherwise we end up with God having favourites, which is not true.

75

'All my love, Mum'

My big brother and I both went to the same boarding school, starting in a preparatory school at the age of eleven, then going to the senior school at twelve. He had been in the senior school three years already before I arrived, and in the early days he used to keep me company some time each day, to make sure I was settling in.

We were together when the first letters from our mother were delivered, the first ones of that term, the first ones to come one each when we were both at the same school. That was a comfort in itself. It could have been that now we were together, one letter would have been thought to be enough, to be shared between us. Instead, we got a letter each.

I can still recall how the long stone corridor felt as we read our letters. At the end of my letter, Mum signed off, 'All my love, Mum.' Panic stations! Why did she go and write a thing like that, with my brother right beside me? My brother got to the end of his letter, and then suggested we swap, to see if there was extra news in the letter we hadn't read yet. My heart sank, but I couldn't refuse.

So I read his letter, and there at the end of it was the solution, so simple. It read, 'All my love, Mum.' Such is the wonder of a mother's love, she can give all of it to every child she has. And as Isaiah says, even if a human mother changed her mind, God won't. Each of us can be the beloved disciple of Jesus, each of us the beloved child of God. There is plenty of room.

76

Good News for saints?

There can be no doubt that the Good News is good for sinners. It is not quite so clear that the news is good for those who have been trying for years to do the right thing. Many practising Christians feel considerable sympathy with the elder brother of the prodigal son. Why does God apparently not value the son who had done everything that was required? Why should God go overboard for someone who evaded all the duties and had all the fun?

The story of the labourers in the vineyard has much the same effect on good people: why should those lazy hounds get the same reward as the others who had slaved away through the heat of the day? This feeling of the righteous is, of course, based on a misunderstanding of their own status. Sinners are often better at knowing their own nakedness before God; they are running away from it. Good people have often clothed their nakedness with clothing that was all along a gift from God, so that they forget their own neediness underneath. It is only when they come to die that they realise they have nothing of their own.

Heaven is for sinners. Saints who wish to enter heaven will have to show that they are sinners (weak, with no power of their own, little children). Sinners will not have to show that they are saints.

My much-used parable will bear repeating here: as I enter the gates of heaven, the first person I see, basking in God's forgiveness, will be the very person I most disapprove of. Then it will be up to me, as it was up to the elder brother, to join in the celebrations over that sinner, or to go some other place. Good people should work well to thank God, not to expect thanks from God.

77

Virtues and vices

We could almost say, 'God will forgive our vices, if we forget our virtues.' It is certainly true that God will forgive our vices if we ask for forgiveness and truly want to do better next time, whether or not we see much chance of success. And it is certainly true that God wants us to forget about our virtues.

In his sermon on the mount Jesus makes a point of the need to keep our virtues secret. In particular he mentions prayer, fasting and alms-deeds, that we take all the good out of them if we do them to be noticed.

The old eucharistic prayer which was recited every day in Catholic churches of the West for seventeen centuries, and which is still one of the options at the Eucharist, asked God to let us into heaven and the company of the saints – and for what reason? Not as a measurer of merit, but as a generous giver-out of pardon. The current translation is a bit more muted: 'Do not consider what we truly deserve, but grant us your forgiveness.'

I marvelled once when I heard someone say he was looking forward to a big generous reward from God for all he had done for the Church. What a sad limit for anyone to put on God's generosity! I hope God does not consider what I truly deserve, which could well turn out to be a minus quantity; I would much rather count on God's generosity, then as always.

Linked with this idea is another saying of Jesus, about not letting our left hand know what our right hand is doing. If our right hand does something good, our left hand is sure to boast about it, given half a chance.

78

God loves us one at a time

One of the greatest differences between the old covenant and the new is that the old was a covenant with the people, whereas the new is a covenant with each and every individual. The individuals then get together and form a community, but one-to-one comes first.

In the history of the Jewish people there were hundreds and thousands who were left behind. Not all Hebrews escaped from Egypt in the first place, not all survived the long ordeal in the desert. Many were killed attempting to conquer the Promised Land; many were killed in wars with the Philistines, trying to hold on to the land. Many more were exiled to Babylon than ever came back. Always the key issue, to us Christians looking back at their history, is that a remnant survived and carried on. From this remnant came the Messiah.

But the Messiah when he came was concerned with individuals. The synagogues at the time frowned on the blind, the lame, the crippled, the deaf, the sinners, the ritually unclean, the foreigners . . . and kept women in the background. Jesus went out of his way to pay attention to each of these, one by one. His healing miracles were performed one by one. He taught us to pray one by one to his *Abba* and ours. His death tore down the veil that kept women and foreigners at a distance. The key reason he was crucified was that he refused to leave any least one of us behind.

So it comes about that the treasures of the old covenant can now be redirected to apply to each and every one of us. In the next three pages, let the reader please feel free to put his or her own name in place of the dots.

79

'This is the word of the Lord about ....' (I)

I made you, ..., in my own image and likeness, and when I made you, I saw that you are good. (cf. Genesis 1:27, 31)

Before the world was made, ..., I chose you, chose you in Christ, to be holy and spotless, and to live through love in my presence. (cf. Ephesians 1:3, 4)

I have loved you, ..., with an everlasting love, and therefore I am constant in my affection for you. (cf. Jeremiah 31:3) I am silently planning for you in love. (cf. Zephaniah 3:17)

Do not be afraid, ..., for I have redeemed you. I have called you by your name, you are mine. You, ..., are precious in my eyes. You are honoured and I love you. (cf. Isaiah 43:1, 4)

I will not forget you, ... I have dispelled your faults like a cloud, your sins like a mist. Come back to me, for I have redeemed you. (cf. Isaiah 44:21f)

I, Christ, loved you, ..., and sacrificed myself for your sake. (cf. Galatians 2:20)

You, ..., are worth more than many sparrows! (cf. Luke 12:7)

You, ..., have become an ambassador for Christ. It is as though I were appealing through you. (cf. 2 Corinthians 5:20)

You, ..., are my friend. (cf. John 15:15)

You, ..., are my work of art (cf. Ephesians 2:10) and part of my household. (cf. Ephesians 2:22)

You, ..., reflect like a mirror the brightness of the Lord, and grow brighter and brighter as you are turned into the image that you reflect: this is my work. (cf. 2 Corinthians 3:18)

I will look after you, ... (cf. Luke 12:28) Your name is branded on the palms of my hands. (cf. Isaiah 49:16)

80

'This is the word of the Lord about ....' (II)

When you were a child, ..., I loved you. I myself taught you to walk, I took you in my arms. Yet, ..., you did not understand that I was the one looking after you. I led you with reins of kindness, with leading strings of love. I was like someone who lifts an infant close against his cheek; stooping down to you, ..., I gave you your food. How could I part with you, how could I give you up? (cf. Hosea 11:1-8)

In the wilderness, ..., I carried you, as a parent carries a child, all along the road you travelled on the way to this place. (cf. Deuteronomy 1:31)

In your old age I shall be the same still, when your hair is grey I shall still support you. I have already done so, ..., I have carried you; I shall still support and deliver you. (cf. Isaiah 46:4)

As a bridegroom rejoices in his bride, so will I, your God, rejoice in you. (cf. Isaiah 62:5)

I will betroth you to myself for ever, ..., betroth you with integrity and justice, with tenderness and love; I will betroth you to myself with faithfulness, and you shall come to know me. (cf. Hosea 2:19-22)

I have gone to prepare a place for you, and I shall return to take you with me, so that where I am, you, ..., may be too. (cf. John 14:2, 3)

I will show you the path of life, ..., the fullness of joy in my presence. (cf. Psalm 16:11)

You have a sure hope, and the promise of an inheritance that can never be spoilt or soiled and never fade away, because it is being kept for you, ..., in the heavens. (cf. 1 Peter 1:4)

I will raise you up, ..., in my power. (cf. 1 Corinthians 6:14)

81

'This is the word of the Lord about ....' (III)

As the Father loved me, so I have loved you, ... (cf. John 15:9)

Have no fear, ..., do not be afraid, have I not told you, ..., and revealed it long ago? (cf. Isaiah 44:8)

You, ..., will rest, with no one to frighten you away. (cf. Isaiah 17:2)

I made a covenant with you, ..., and you became mine. (cf. Ezekiel 16:8)

No disaster can overtake you, ...; I rescue you, ..., who cling to me; I protect you, ..., who know my name; I am with you, ..., when you are in trouble. (cf. Psalm 91:10-15)

As one whom the mother caresses, ..., so will I comfort you. (cf. Isaiah 66:13)

You are my servant, ...; I have chosen you, not rejected you. (cf. Isaiah 41:9)

I am your Father, ..., and you are clay. I am your maker, ..., and you, the work of my hands. (cf. Isaiah 64:8)

You, ..., shall run and not be weary, you shall walk and not faint. (cf. Isaiah 40:31)

Look to me, ..., that you may be radiant with joy. (cf. Psalm 34:5)

I will forgive your iniquity, ..., and remember your sin no more. (cf. Jeremiah 31:34)

You, ..., will draw waters joyfully from the springs of salvation. (cf. Isaiah 12:3)

Come to me, ..., you who labour and are heavily burdened, and I will refresh you. (cf. Matthew 11:28)

82

The jigsaw puzzle

If you have ever tried to play a game of cards with only 51 cards in the pack, you will know how impossible it all becomes. In theory you can take a card from another pack, if you have another pack, but then the new one stands out as different when the cards are dealt and everyone knows who has that particular card and the game is spoiled.

Similarly if you have ever drawn closer and closer to completing a jigsaw puzzle with 1,000 pieces, only to find there are now only 999 pieces, you will know the frustration of it. Who cares if the missing piece is a vital part of the picture, like the hour hand of the clock Big Ben or the tip of King Arthur's sword, or whether it is a piece of nondescript sky or grass or treetop . . . the frustration is in the fact of its spoiling the completeness of a long-lasting task.

Jesus leaves us in no doubt that he regards each one of us as being just as important to the completion of his task as the one piece of jigsaw is vital to the puzzle. By teaching us all equally to call God our *Abba* he has turned the whole human race into a family affair, and in a family everybody counts as much as everybody else. If you have ever known a family where one of the children died young, you will remember how the family is never the same again for the parents: their sadness is never completely removed by the other children, however loving the rest of the children may be.

Jesus gives the example of the man with 100 sheep who loses one: no matter which it is, he goes to enormous lengths to get that precious one back.

83

Treasure in the field

With the advent of metal detectors, more and more fields are turning out to have treasure hidden in them. Only the other day, as I write this, a farmer's son unearthed over 9,000 Roman silver coins, mostly *denarii*, in a field in Somerset. He did not need to go away and buy the field like the man in Jesus' parable: it was his father's field already. The rules were evidently different in Jesus' time and place: here and now it makes no real difference who owns the field, but we can see what Jesus is meaning. If we find something of eternal value, we should go for it with everything we have.

These days I find myself comparing 'the field' to 'the Church'. In the field there would be hectares upon hectares of earth, with or without crops growing, stony or arable, fit for sheep or for cattle or fit for nothing. Jesus does not say. So, too, in the Church there is a lot else which is not treasure. In my own case, I had been 24 years in the Church as a member before the priceless value of the Good News dawned on me. I found the treasure. Now to me it would be senseless to complain at all bitterly about the field, the Church, since I found the treasure there. I buy the field, treasure and all, even though the treasure is only part of the package.

Because I believe that we each have our own window on the world, I also believe that we each have our own field for the buying. In my world I found the priceless treasure in the Church, in the gospels and the family life and the sacraments and the friendship and the healing which finally led to the dawning of God's unending love for me and therefore for everyone else. So I could not ever dissuade anyone else from looking in their 'field' for the same treasure.

84

Pearl of great price

The parable about the treasure in the field has a 'twin', which is the parable about the merchant looking for fine pearls. When he finds one of superb value he sells everything and buys that pearl. This time there is no extra package coming along with the pearl, just the pearl. Either the merchant is going to make a huge profit on it when the market improves, like a modern-day investor collecting masterpieces of art, or else he will simply keep it to admire and wonder at.

The most obvious application to the spiritual life is that all other things we treasure are worth trading in for the one thing that is necessary. In fact most of the currency which we trade in for the Good News is bad news, so there is no comparison. I have already twice in these pages listed the sort of things: anxiety, judgement, competition, jealousy, etc. – all things we can well do without. We are enormously the gainers if we have instead the personal love of God for us whether or not we are making a success of our lives.

Perhaps as an added lustre to the pearl we might think of it as being a crystal ball or a wishing-well and not just a pearl. We can look into the precious stone we possess and see the stories of the gospels coming to life. There is Jesus coming to me when I am feeling cut off from humanity, saying, 'Of course I want to heal you', and welcoming me into his company. There he is, sitting me next to him at his supper. There he is, telling me my sins are forgiven. There he is, inviting me to walk with him. There he is, asleep in my boat, so why need I be afraid? There he is, telling me that he and I are children of God, not liable to pay tax, but that I can help him if I will.

85

'Do not be afraid'

The last book I wrote had 'Do not be afraid' for a title. What started me on that book was a saying I read somewhere, that there were 365 times in the Bible that it tells us, or someone, not to be afraid. I went looking, and found there were two-hundred-and-something times, but that there were easily enough encouraging things said in the Bible to select one for each day of the year.

I wrote the book in a random order, not following any special pattern of themes, but in fact the 'Do not be afraid' passages do come under certain headings. There are those that remind us to be little children before God; there are those that remind us God has looked after us thus far along our journey through life, and that therefore God is not likely to give us up as a bad job now. We are reminded many times not to be afraid of storms, not just the physical storms like the one when Jesus was in the boat with his disciples, but the inner storms that afflict all of us from time to time.

Jesus has compassion on our sickness, and God is always a God of compassion. Soldiers wounded in battle need never be ashamed of their wounds, and neither need we be ashamed of our physical or spiritual ills when we show them to Jesus our healer. We need never even be ashamed of our failures, since Jesus, like the Good Samaritan, will come by and pick us up and heal us very willingly. He wants us back on form as soon as possible. If we feel we have failed as shepherds looking after his flock, he treats us as a good shepherd treats a slightly inefficient sheepdog, and gets the sheep into the pen himself. He is glad that we tried. He tells us not to be afraid of persecutions, not to be afraid of loneliness, since some loneliness is the price we pay for being unique.

86

'Ah, but what about . . . ?'

When I give a talk or a sermon about the Good News, it quite often happens that someone comes up afterwards and says, 'Yes, that sounds very comforting, and I would love to believe it. But what about . . . ?' Then they refer to the sheep being separated from the goats, or some vision of Teresa of Avila about souls going down to hell like leaves in autumn or like snowflakes, or it may be they simply have a resentment about all the people who do not care about religion, while they themselves have always tried very hard. I have tried to deal with that last complaint already, since it is the problem of the elder brother of the prodigal. But from now on in this book I will take some of the other ideas that make people doubt the Good News, one by one.

First, however, a general principle. Do we accept the story of the prodigal son as being from Jesus? Do we accept the words of Jesus to the good thief as being authentic? Do we believe, with St John, that God is love, and, with Paul, that love is always patient and kind?

If we do believe, then anything in the Bible – New Testament or Old – that seems to contradict that basic compassion cannot be from God. If I find myself being treated without mercy by the Bible at any stage, then I have either misunderstood it, or else Jesus has superseded it and I need no longer be afraid. The idea of all the good people going to heaven and all the sinners going to hell is an Old Testament notion or a notion that simply comes from human unforgivingness. As an idea it was around long before Jesus, and it is still around now. We do tend to slide back from the Good News. Judgement is not the Good News. So, are we going to cling on to what was pre-Jesus, or listen to Jesus?

87

Field with corn and weeds

Matthew's gospel gives us Jesus' parable about the man who sowed good wheat seed in his field, and then an enemy came and sowed darnel seed on top of the wheat seed. People today argue about what plant exactly it was that the enemy sowed, but we know from the way the story develops that the weed was probably of a clinging, parasite variety, since it could not be pulled out without pulling out the growing wheat as well. (cf. Matthew 13:24-30)

In Matthew's gospel there follows an explanation of the parable (13:36-40), which does not treat Jesus' story as a parable but as an allegory. It says, amongst other things, that the good wheat equals the good people, and the bad seed equals the bad people, who will end up in the furnace. The trouble with that explanation is that it contradicts Jesus' usual teaching and practice, and it tells us nothing that human nature did not already fear. It is not Good News.

However, taking Jesus' story on its own, the most striking novelty about it is that the landowner is patient, whereas his servants are in too much of a hurry. If we recognise that Jesus deals with individuals, then any one person can say, 'That field is me. There is good in me and there are faults or sins in me. The one who owns this field (God) is not in any urgent hurry to pull out the weeds in me, lest it harm the good in me. Rather like a teacher who does not break the spirit of the pupils by pointing to every little mistake, God wants me to carry on doing the best I can; at the finish I will be able to leave behind my faults and sins, and only the good in me will live on with me.' Now that sounds more like the Jesus we know, who is all for giving sinners another chance.

88

The third man

There are two versions of the parable of the talents, one in Matthew and one in Luke. They differ in details, but as regards the point I wish to make they amount to the same. In each of them there is a third character who hides his talent or his *mina* (worth 100 denarii) and does nothing with it, then gets condemned by the one who lent the money in the first place.

If we are not careful we can find ourselves thinking that the picture of God that Jesus gives is a two-faced God, praising and rewarding the successful and damning the failures. In fact, it gives two images of God, one of which is true and the other of which is false.

If we are convinced that God is like 'a hard man, picking up what he has not put down, and reaping what he has not sown', then we will shrivel up. If, in other words, we decide that God is bad news rather than Good News, we will not take God on as an employer; we will not take any risks. We will try to play safe, resort to excuses, hide ourselves from God. Whereas if we decide God is Good News, we will take risks, knowing that God will always make allowances should things not work out as planned.

These two parables are not so much about what happens at the final judgement as about the here and now and the judgements that we make every day. Reality is such that if we believe the ultimate reality is forgiveness, we will blossom in the things that really matter. But if we believe the ultimate reality is judgement, we will never be really happy. We will be basing our lives on a lie.

89

The kingdom of forgiveness

I want now to return briefly to the story of the man who was let off a debt of 10,000 talents, but who then went and spoiled everything for himself by not forgiving a fellow servant a debt of 100 denarii. There is in Jesus' stories and parables a certain feeling of 'You must', which sounds as if Jesus is putting conditions on God's love. There are in fact no conditions on God's love and forgiveness, but Jesus does clearly imply that if we do not try to forgive others, we blind ourselves to the fact of God's forgiving us, so that as far as we are concerned it might as well not be true.

If I may quote again from an old book of mine now out of print:

The kingdom of heaven means living in God's way, breathing God's air, thinking God's thoughts, living like the child of a particular Father. God is a kind of living. Jesus revealed his Father to us. So in fact every day I walk in and out of the kingdom of heaven, as my thoughts and my actions come closer to God or move further from God.

The difference is that God's world is everlasting, and outside of that atmosphere all is perishable, so we do well to stay in God's air. And God's order of things includes total acceptance of every person living. If I exclude anyone from my esteem, to that extent I shut myself out from God's esteem; if I shut out anyone from my love, to that extent I shut myself out from God's love. God loves and forgives the one I refuse to forgive, so where does that leave me? Nowhere but on the outside.

I cannot choose blue sky for me and black clouds for someone else. The measure we give is the measure we get. If we choose a judgemental god, that is the god who will rule our lives.

90

A hundredfold

There are needless fears lurking in the parables about the sower and the wheat. Supposing I am one of those along the path, doomed to barrenness, or one of those sown on rocky ground, doomed to give up at the crucial moment; or one of those sown among thorns and thistles: I have enough worldly cares, are they stifling all the good in me? Even if I qualify as good soil, will I manage a 100 per cent increase, or will I only manage an average 60 per cent, or a near failure mark at 30 per cent? Jesus, like any teacher, can find it difficult to say things in a way that *nobody* will take up wrongly!

The prime example of seed falling on the path is Peter. He had no sooner accepted the word that Jesus is the Christ, than Satan came and took it away from him: he could accept a successful Messiah, but not one who was going to end up on a cross. 'Get behind me, Satan!' said Jesus to Peter. Yet Peter is now in heaven, we may safely believe. The prime example of seed falling on stony ground is the pair of brothers, James and John, full of fire until the real crisis came. But they are now both reckoned to be saints. All of the Twelve were mixed up about the value of riches, thinking that riches are a sign of God's approval. But that did not stop them from becoming foundation stones of Jesus' Church.

The seed is the word of God which says that we are God's children. The sower sows it; it stays in the dark in the ground; we learn to give it growing space; it grows secretly; in the end it takes over our whole life, and makes us a shelter for others. Whether we are like ducks with twelve ducklings or dandelions making a hundred new dandelions, that is up to God.

91

The narrow gate

One may occasionally come across a crucifix or a painting of the crucifixion in which the arms of Jesus reach almost directly above his head. This kind of image of the cross was favoured by the Jansenists, on the rather bizarre reasoning that Jesus thus fits through the narrow door better than with his arms stretched wide to embrace the whole human race.

When Jesus tells his disciples to strive to enter by the narrow door, and to be among the few who do so, is he saying that not many will be saved by his life and death? Given that God is love, and that the story of the good thief is true, how can we take Jesus' words about the narrow door in some other way?

The way that I understand it is this: there were only twelve disciples actively involved with Jesus in the feeding of the five thousand (not counting women and children!), yet there were five thousand and more people fed. There was one chief shepherd, twelve under-shepherds (or sheepdogs) and thousands cared for. In the list I gave, of the two sides of the gospel, there will always be more fish than there are fishers, more coins than coin-seekers, more Marthas than Marys. Jesus is offering us the privilege of working with him, a privilege that will always involve the cross, so there is a considerable reluctance to join his disciples. The five thousand could all go home to their families when the day was done; the twelve disciples could not: they were hooked.

Many are called to become wholehearted Christians: the offer is open to all. But not as many take up the offer. If they only knew the value of the treasure in the field, there would be more.

92

Dictators and despots

One obvious stumbling-block in many people's minds, when it comes to trying to forgive everyone the way God does, is that there are some human beings who appear to us to be monsters. How can we ever be expected to share heaven with them and forgive them? Not just the dictators and despots, but the child-killers, the torturers, the bullies, the vandals who have destroyed something precious to us, the burglars who desecrated our home? The list could be endless. The bombers who blew up a family, the bombers who blew a planeload of innocent people out of the sky. Surely God could not expect us to forgive the likes of these?

There are a few lines of thought that might help here. The horrors such people cause usually affect a whole community, and the community in the end helps the families most involved to come to terms with what has happened and carry on with their lives.

Jesus says, more or less in parallel, that we should forgive our enemies and that we should pray for them. If we cannot get the bitterness out of our hearts, at least we can pray for those who hurt us. Even if we only pray that they stop doing what they are doing, that no one will follow or imitate them, that they will see the horror of what they have done and be sorry.

It is good when the news media pick up on a family that has decided not to hate the murderers of their loved ones. The ultimate reason we should forgive everyone is hard to take, but is true: what one human being does, any other human being is capable of. Jesus died for human nature.

93

Why then be good?

There is a very human reaction against the preaching of the Good News as good news. 'If God loves everybody all the time, why should we bother to try and do the right thing by one another? Why not just grab all we can here and now, and enjoy heaven as well, according to you? What you are teaching is the death-knell for all morality.'

These were the reasons why Jesus was killed, so if a preacher of the Good News is criticised on those grounds, then he or she is in the best of company. Even today when in the Sunday liturgy it comes round to the turn of the story of the labourers in the vineyard or the return of the lost son, there is a groundswell of sympathy for the labourers who had worked all day, and for the elder brother.

In actual fact, knowing how good and forgiving God is does not stunt the growth of good works. Zacchaeus is the shining example in the stories about Jesus: he was forgiven everything and responded by going way beyond the requirements of the law. I must say, too, that in my own case learning how good and forgiving God is has not in any way made me want to sit back and do nothing. Since that day 41 years ago I have done all that I would in any case have done for God, and done it with infinitely more enthusiasm. If anything, at one stage I overdid my zeal and became quite ill.

Why bother preaching the Good News if God is likely to forgive us all for everything anyway? Because otherwise so many will turn up face to face with God when they die, and discover for the first time, so late, that they need never have run away from God all those years, leaving pain and disaster in their wake.

94

'Didn't God create the devil?'

This question used to bother me, and I still hear people putting the same question to me as an objection to the way I tell the Good News. How could a God so good create a world which was not immune from such an evil creature?

To come straight to my own solution to the problem: I found it in the *Concise Theological Dictionary* of Father Karl Rahner, surely a most reliable theologian, and a book complete with *Imprimatur* and *Nihil obstat* from the Catholic diocese in which it was published. Devils and demons, according to Rahner, are the powers of this world. Evil is personal because it is only found in persons, evil is not extra-persons wandering round looking to create trouble. In effect, we do not have to believe in the devil as an extra-person keeping an evil eye on us. The ones we have to watch are ourselves.

But still comes the question: why did God create us with a potential for evil? This is mainly to do with free will: if we are free, we are free to do the wrong thing. And, so often, evil comes out of misunderstanding, people not taking the best interpretation of what is said or done to them. One of the old Laurel and Hardy short comedy films is almost a parable of original sin. In *The Christmas Tree Sellers* the pair take a Christmas tree off their lorry and take it to the door of a house. They are house-to-house sales-men. The house owner opens the door, sees them, says he doesn't want any Christmas trees today, and shuts the door. The tip of the tree is caught in the top of the door as it slams. The pair look at one another, then knock at the door again. From then on the anger escalates on both sides, tit for tat, until the man's house is a wreck and the trees and the lorry are all destroyed.

95

Judas

The writings and documents of the Church over the centuries have never said that Judas is in hell. That in itself is remarkable, since it is only relatively recently that Christians who committed suicide were allowed a Christian burial in a Christian cemetery. The Roman Catholic *Order of Christian Funerals* currently in use dates from 1970 and is the first one I have come across with official rites and prayers for those who have killed themselves, though the sympathetic attitude to individuals goes back much longer than that, of course.

What has always upset me, and still does to some extent, is the way Jesus says, 'For the Son of Man goes as it is written of him, but woe to that one by whom the Son of Man is betrayed! It would be better for that one not to have been born.' But does he only mean Judas? The saying is placed by Mark at the Last Supper, just before Judas betrayed Jesus, but we know the gospel writers often chose their own setting for a saying of Jesus that might have been spoken at some other time. The saying about betrayal does not use our word 'man', meaning 'male person'; it uses the word *anthropos*, which means 'member of the human race'. Perhaps the best way to take the saying is to see each one of us as capable of betraying Jesus. I know I am quite capable of it. I am only worthy to carry on because I am a child of God, not just a human child.

Consoling in this respect is the way Jesus elsewhere says that 'Those who are ashamed of me and of my words in this adulterous and sinful generation, of them the Son of Man will also be ashamed when he comes in the glory of his Father with the holy angels.' Peter was ashamed of Jesus at the fire in the high priest's courtyard, yet Jesus did not disown him, then or ever.

96

The sheep and the goats

This is a favourite story quoted by people who find the Good News too risky to believe in. Surely, they say, Jesus is quite adamant that the sheep are the good people and they go to heaven, whereas the goats are the bad people and they go to hell for all eternity?

Well, for a start, if that was all Jesus came to tell us, he was telling the human race nothing it did not already believe. Further, and more importantly, it is impossible for us to identify anyone around us as 100 per cent sheep or 100 per cent goat. Beginning with myself, as we should do rather than judge other people, I have not done much physical feeding or giving to drink at all. I have done some prison visiting of one sort or another, but I have not made it a regular practice. I have visited some sick people, certainly, but failed to visit a whole lot of others I knew were ill. I have only given oddments of good clothing away. I have welcomed many strangers and tried to be tolerant, but in the busy retreat house where I live I have often taken a detour to avoid meeting yet more people. So what am I, a sheep or a goat? What will the shepherd do with me? Surely the point of the story is to list the things that count, that we should be doing. Jesus lines himself up with every sufferer in the world, and says, 'If you leave that one behind, you leave me behind. You will have to come back and fetch us.'

If the good thief had met Jesus two years earlier, and asked him, 'Master, what should I do?', Jesus would have told him about the sheep and the goats. But if two years later the thief had confessed to Jesus he had never got round to doing those things, and still asked for pity, he would have received it, as in fact happened.

97

Chorazin, Bethsaida and Capernaum

The only claim to fame of the city of Chorazin is that it was severely strictured by Jesus, along with Capernaum, which was his original base of operations in Galilee, and Bethsaida which was a fishing town at the north end of the lake, where Philip, Peter and Andrew came from and where Jesus cured a blind man. Capernaum is a surprise in this context, since it does seem that Capernaum was enthusiastic about the work of Jesus. One time early on, according to Mark's gospel, Jesus had to re-enter the town secretly because of all the excitement his presence was causing; and when he was discovered at the house of Peter, crowds filled the house and overflowed on to the street.

At all events, Matthew's and Luke's gospels recount Jesus saying, 'Woe to you, Chorazin!', 'Woe to you, Bethsaida!' and also 'Woe to you, Capernaum!' His reason is that the famously wicked cities of old, Tyre and Sidon and even Sodom, would have repented long ago if they had seen the deeds of power that had been done by Jesus. Jesus then seems to assign these three currently blind towns to Hades in the day of judgement, because they could not see the obvious.

But when is the day of judgement? One certain fact is that if these three towns could not accept Jesus' word as true on the strength of his deeds of power, then they were left in their unredeemed status as regards God. They would never in this life know that they were first-generation children of God, forgiven, cherished, and called to be ambassadors of that Good News to the rest of the world. Even in the final day of judgement they would not be 'top of the league' as the towns that gave the Son of God to the world, but they would be for ever the towns that missed the boat.

98

Ten bridesmaids

One of my teachers of scripture many years ago was a Flemish priest who was very friendly with the local Jewish community where he lived. He used to talk over with them the stories about Jesus and the stories Jesus told. When it came to the story of the ten bridesmaids, five of them foolish and five of them wise, the Jewish friends immediately showed how Jesus the rabbi would have presented such a story. Five wise bridesmaids: up goes the right hand of Jesus with five fingers showing. Five foolish ones: up goes the left hand, five fingers showing.

If that was the starting point of the story, the whole parable takes on a different feel. Like the one about the sheep and the goats, or the weeds in the field of good wheat, this too can be seen as a picture of any human being, this time with a right hand which is skilful and a left hand which is clumsy (or vice versa in the case of left-handed people), and, more significantly, any human being who has dreams of being great and good but who at the same time is dragged back by limitations of moral weakness. Once more, as in those other parables, we end up with not the wise people going to heaven and the foolish ones going to hell, but with an urgent message to spread the wisdom throughout our one life, rather than let the folly prevail.

There is always the secret feeling that the 'wise' bridesmaids were acting in a very un-Christian way! When we ask ourselves what is the meaning of the oil in the lamps that is so necessary, surely it is our faith that Jesus would never leave the least of his little ones outside his love. Indeed he himself died outside the walls of Jerusalem for that very reason.

99

The wedding garment

There are two versions of the parable of the wedding feast in the gospels, one in Matthew and one in Luke. A king advertised a wedding banquet for his son, or just 'someone' gave a great dinner and sent out invitations. In Luke's story, the first people invited gave various excuses, and the 'someone' was angry, inviting instead the poor, the crippled, the blind and the lame out of the streets and lanes of the town. When the house was still not full, he sent his slaves outside the town into the roads and lanes to compel whoever they met to come to the banquet. Those invited first were not invited a second time.

In Matthew's story the king reacted violently against the first refusers, even destroying them and burning their city. His slaves were sent out into the streets to gather all people they found, good and bad alike, till the wedding hall was filled with guests. Then in Matthew's version comes the tail-piece about the wedding garment. One of the guests was not wearing a wedding garment, and had no excuse. He was thrown out. What is that supposed to mean to us?

What about the wedding garment? To me it is perfectly plain that many wedding garments must have been sitting there at the entrance to the wedding hall, caftans for all comers to pick up and put on. This one character had not bothered, thought he was well enough dressed already. This must be the case, because otherwise we have the picture of half the town at the street corners, and all the travellers and tramps of the surrounding countryside (a) possessing a wedding garment in case of sudden need, and (b) happening to have it with them when bundled into the feast. And what in our terms is the garment? Surely, it is God's forgiveness. It is ours, if we only consent to wear it.

100

Better believe it

Accepting the Good News is a gamble. For human beings, forgiveness is a gamble. No one can prove to you or to me that forgiveness is the ultimate reality. We have to believe it first, and step into the banquet before we know for certain that it is real. Jesus staked his life on forgiveness: he was plotted against and killed because he taught that God loves and forgives and welcomes sinners. He went to his death forgiving those who brought about his crucifixion. To the first teacher of Christian forgiveness, this was no parlour game, but a gamble on which he staked his very life. So now, if we believe him, we have to be the first to unclench our fists in a confrontation. We have to believe that peace is possible.

All I can add on this last page, is that *it works*. Life is infinitely better if we believe that God is love and love is endlessly patient and kind, and if we reorganise our lives and our thinking on that basis. It would be nice if we could all have the experience of seeing Jesus risen *first*, and then going on to live a Christian life of love and tolerance. In fact it usually works the other way round. We take a chance on Jesus actually meaning what he says and does, and bit by bit we find that it works. Some people then, like St Ignatius Loyola my patron, reach the stage where even if the Bible and history books all disappeared they would still believe in all Jesus taught, because they have seen it for themselves and seen him for themselves. For most of us the process is more gradual, but it is none the less like a coming home. The scenery of the world and its relationships clicks together like the 'dry bones' of Ezekiel, and that in itself is part of the Resurrection. I can only encourage my readers to try the wedding garment on for size, if they have not already done so.

CHRISTIANS
IN POLITICS

Published under licence by Brown Dog Books and
The Self-Publishing Partnership Ltd, 10b Greenway Farm, Bath Rd,
Wick, nr. Bath BS30 5RL

www.selfpublishingpartnership.co.uk

ISBN printed book: 978-1-83952-389-2
ISBN e-book: 978-1-83952-390-8

Cover design by Kevin Rylands
Internal design by Andrew Easton

Printed and bound in the UK

This book is printed on FSC certified paper